Hiring and Retaining Top IT Professionals
The Guide for Savvy Hiring Managers and Job Hunters Alike

Hiring and Retaining Top IT Professionals
The Guide for Savvy Hiring Managers and Job Hunters Alike

Howard Adamsky

Osborne/**McGraw-Hill**

New York Chicago San Francisco Lisbon London Madrid Mexico City
Milan New Dehli San Juan Seoul Singapore Sydney Toronto

Osborne/**Mcgraw-Hill**
2600 Tenth Street
Berkeley, California 94710
U.S.A.

To arrange bulk purchase discounts for sales promotions, premiums, or fund-raisers, please contact Osborne/**Mcgraw-Hill** at the above address. For information on translations or book distributors outside the U.S.A., please see the International Contact Information page immediately following the index.

Hiring and Retaining Top IT Professionals:
The Guide for Savvy Hiring Managers and Job Hunters Alike

1234567890 DOC DOC 01987654321

ISBN 0-07-219098-1

Publisher	**Developmental Editor**
Brandon A. Nordin	Paul Greenberg
Vice President & Associate Publisher	**Proofreader**
Scott Rogers	Andrea Fox
Editorial Director	**Indexer**
Roger Stewart	Jack Lewis
Project Manager	**Computer Designer**
Deidre Dolce	Maureen Forys, Happenstance Type-O-Rama
Freelance Project Manager	
Laurie Stewart	**Series Design**
Acquisitions Coordinators	Maureen Forys, Happenstance Type-O-Rama
Alissa Larson	
Timothy Madrid	**Cover Design**
Copy Editor	Egad Dzyn
Sachi Guzman	

This book was composed with QuarkXPress 4.11 on a Macintosh G4.

To Bill, Jake, and Nick. Three great sons.

To Corinne, my wife and best friend, whose courage and positive belief that tomorrow will be better than today is a blessing to her often dark, temperamental, and moody husband.

To M.R., my first loss and M.S., Jake's first loss. Both gone at 18 for no good reason and both remembered with affection, admiration, and awe. Clearly examples of God's inability to exercise the judgment and fairness we all hope for but often cannot find.

To the memory of Zachary Tripp and to Ray Tripp III, M.D., who have always been there for us. I wish you peace.

Contents at a Glance

Contents

Foreword

For 30 years, I built and ran an advertising agency. It grew from an innocent (and presumptuous) one-man proprietorship into a company billing hundreds of millions of dollars with a corresponding cadre of hundreds of employees. Here are the three things I learned—and not always the easy way—about the importance of hiring intelligently.

1. *Hiring is casting.* You aren't hiring an independent operator; you are hiring a critical component of a multi-faceted society. The question isn't how singularly talented a candidate might be, it's how he or she will elevate the resident skills of the existing team, as well as that group's efficiency, motivation, and happiness. And just as in a Broadway production, the tone and energy of the effort will be set by a few key players. Each cast member fulfills a necessary role, but not everyone can be a star.

2. *The critical hires come early.* If continuous, profitable growth is your company's objective (and why would you want to work anyplace where it isn't?), early hires tend to semi-automatically metamorphose into roles of departmental leadership. If you begin with A-level leaders, they fearlessly will hire A-level team members. But Bs will hire Cs who will hire Ds until the degenerative mediocrity is ubiquitous.

3. *Sustained success is a direct function of company culture.* A company's institutionalized culture, good and bad, will be expressed in everything its workforce does. New hires learn their business practices from both supervisors and peers, and experienced new employees arrive with ingrained habits. It is essential, therefore, that every company articulate the principles for which it stands, that *all* its managers live the company's philosophies, and that new employees learn these lessons osmotically—through every memo, hallway conversation, and action of its leadership, especially its senior executives.

It is worth contemplating the last point carefully. I often told clients that the words *Chief Executive Officer* on my business card were misleading. In fact, I ran an operational unit: The Department of Environment and Standards. The philosophies, policies, and practices that my managers and I instituted, taught, reinforced, and personally observed became the unwritten bible of the company. New employees who shared them would become long-term, loyal colleagues, and those who didn't would leave, one way or the other.

Once, when we were about a 100-person agency, I remember shocking a consultant by declining the opportunity to pitch a huge piece of new business.

"Why not?" he asked. "This could be your big break."

"Because if we are successful," I replied, "I'd immediately have to hire 75 people I don't know, and we'd never be the same company again."

During the great dot com business explosion, cultural dilution undermined a lot of good companies. On an organizational level, growth was easy, seductive, and irresistible. But on a national level, the runaway economy quickly dried up the labor pool, causing a discouraging number of organizations to inflate their average salaries, ramp up benefits, and— worst of all—offer new employees advantages (options, stretched vacations, etc.) that were unavailable to the existing workforce. The message this shouted to in-place employees was clear, even to veterans with a deep sense of commitment: The company that asked you to care about it doesn't really care all that much about you, so move on.

We all witnessed the dot com economy's abrupt crash to earth, but the lessons it taught workers left a permanent mark on hiring practices. For better or worse (it's some of each), talented individuals learned that their skills are mobile: Job stability is nothing to be cherished, and job change is nothing to be feared. Virtually no skilled person today joins a company with the intention of lifetime service. Yet, perhaps ironically, organizations now have a greater need than ever to nurture a culture that encourages employee longevity. While money will always remain the scorecard, valuable employees are poignantly aware of *demonstrated* corporate appreciation, and compare job advantages and disadvantages in many categories.

In this book, Howard Adamsky teaches responsible techniques for effective hiring, offering unique insights into a workforce world transformed forever by employee impermanence. His recommended hiring practices are the first key steps in a successful business mutualism—a relationship in which both parties, employee and employer, contribute elementally to each other's well being. A fair, considerate, and effective hiring experience will lead the way to an enlightened, employee-oriented culture.

Life is a long dance, and employee/employer relationships are better enjoyed as waltzes than boogaloos.

—Jim Mullen

Founder and former CEO of Mullen Advertising, an advertising, public relations, and interactive marketing firm

Preface

I am not much of a researcher. The part of my brain that controls that function does very little heavy lifting. As a result, I try to compensate with the other side of my brain—the creative side—that is more artistic and imaginative. I say this up front because if you are looking for statistics, charts, graphs, and data, you are barking up the wrong tree. By design, this is not that type of book. Instead, I hope you find this book more interesting and enlightening because it is a collection of all I have seen and been involved in since the beginning of my consulting practice. After all, statistics and studies, which we worship as a culture, can be limiting. They so often contradict each other and usually speak to us about what we already know, not what we should *do*.

Between its covers, the words in this book represent my beliefs, ideas, values, standards, opinions, and yes…my solutions. The world according to me? Not exactly. But it is a clear guide to the pitfalls and landmines that interfere with our ability to attract and retain exceptional talent, and a roadmap to guide you toward success. Although this book focuses on the IT community, the contents can be applied to virtually any industry concerned with hiring and retaining talented people. The principles found within these pages will, if applied judiciously, add great value to your organization by supporting your efforts in creating a stronger, more functional, and highly cohesive workforce. I present the information in such a way that the reader follows the natural progression of events that normally take place in the building of a company.

Chapter 1 deals with planning. It is vital to anticipate and plan for growth by hiring more people. In the fast-paced world of technology, planning is sometimes put on the back burner because speed to market is the all-important goal. Having lived in the world of technology for many years, I am well aware of the importance of speed. I simply urge the reader to understand that planning is the road that speed travels on. Plan your course of action well, otherwise the old saying, "Never time to do it right but always time to do it twice" might easily become your reality. And doing it twice really does slow you down.

Chapter 2 describes the candidate generation process. Numerous candidate generation methodologies exist. There is no doubt that the Internet will rule the roost for a long time to come, but do not see it as the magic bullet. Many other options are available to you for finding candidates.

Chapter 3 addresses the next logical step in the hiring process: Interviewing the candidates you generated. I give the reader insight into the importance of proper interviewing and how to get the most out of this process that is a mixture of art and science. Everyone can learn how to become effective and thorough interviewers. The key to your success lies in your commitment to learning the process well.

Chapter 4 was the most difficult to write. How do I advise you on who should or shouldn't get a job offer? You can discuss the pros and cons of a candidate ad nauseam, but sooner or later, someone has to make the decision. It is impossible to teach someone, through a book or any other method, the judgment required to make the right decisions on hiring. However, I can provide insight on how to avoid costly mistakes. All of us make bad hires. The objective is to make as few as possible, thereby saving the company and the candidate a good deal of time and effort.

Chapter 5 has to do with the chase. Once you make an offer, you have to close the deal. You have to land the candidate in spite of competing offers and counteroffers. You won't always win these battles. But, use some of the strategies I describe, and you will win just as many as the competition.

Chapter 6 is the granddaddy of them all. It deals with employee retention, which plays as large a role in building your organization as hiring itself. Good employees are assets you can't afford to lose. This chapter attempts to move the reader away from using gimmicks and fad-oriented techniques as a method of retaining employees. People will stay with your organization far more for what the organization is at its core than for pizza lunches and casual Fridays.

Chapter 7 is titled "Notes from the Underground." It is a collection of thoughts and recommendations I feel strongly about that didn't fit neatly into the preceding chapters. The range of topics is wide, the opinions strong. Reflecting upon his body of work, John Updike recently said, "I guess I have had my say." "Notes from the Underground" is the opportunity for me to have mine.

For those who wish to discuss this book, its ideas, concepts, or philosophy, feel free to call my office at 978-897-8500, day or night. Or, if you want to talk motorcycles or you live in the Boston area and want to lose in a paddleball game, you can call me, on that issue as well.

—Howard Adamsky
Stow, MA
June 3, 2001

Acknowledgments

"Come, my friends,
'Tis not too late to seek a newer world."

—Tennyson

A first book is an interesting thing…it also has the potential of being the last. Hopefully, that is not *my* fate. I wrote this book because I have much to say about the work I do, and I firmly believe my efforts have made a difference. Freud said there is only work and love. Without either, there is neurosis. I have all three. Therefore, in case this *is* to be my last book, please allow me the opportunity to thank all the people who have helped me get to this most interesting place in my life.

Loosely defined, acknowledgments generally exist so the author can thank those who supported the writing of the book. In most cases, these people are individuals with whom the author has actually had some contact. Never having been a slave to convention, I would like to do it differently. I want to take the time, and space, to acknowledge people who helped me simply because they exist and cared enough to put pen to paper. Their actions enhanced and expanded my awareness, left their mark on my psyche, and opened my mind to things I'd never given any serious consideration.

Willie Nelson sings that his heroes have always been cowboys. Coming from Brooklyn, New York, I am not all that familiar with cowboys. My heroes have always been writers and thinkers and doers. With that in mind, let me express the following heartfelt thanks to some of my heroes.

My sincerest thanks to Arthur Cavanaugh, my friend, whose novel, *Leaving Home*, is one of the five best books I ever read. A book I couldn't put down and will never forget. It is, in the words of Taylor Caldwell, "Haunting." Mr. Cavanaugh and I spent two hours speaking at length in his New York apartment. I will never forget that day.

My sincerest thanks to Joseph Heller who wrote *Catch–22*, and reaffirmed my belief that the world is every bit as absurd as I imagined. And more, I drove 500 miles to meet Mr. Heller and managed to procure (don't ask how) the last ticket to a private reading for his next to last book, *Now and Then*. We spoke for a few moments. The bright lights that lit him for the television cameras illuminated him from behind, and his untamed gray hair took on the luminescence of gold. It was a great moment for me. Joseph Heller died trying to recreate the greatness that was in *Catch-22*. This was neither possible nor necessary. Even if he never wrote anything else afterward, his place in literature is secure. (By the way, his book *Something Happened* is a must read, full of the dark and "Helleresque" humor that is so immediately identifiable. It is perhaps more relevant today than when originally written.)

I would also like to thank James Hilton for teaching me about kindness, John Gunther for teaching me about courage, Ray Bradbury for teaching me about conviction, and Rod Serling and H.G. Wells for helping me to understand that I will never comprehend the concept of time—what it is, where it goes, or how to slow its pace. Their books have inspired me in a way that can only come from pain, suffering, despair, and courage. Their ability to start with a blank page, and then say what they must so eloquently, is a talent of which I am in awe.

Most people are more than willing to tell you all the things you can't possibly do in your life. If you listen to them enough, you begin to believe it yourself. My sincerest thanks to Zig Ziggler, Les Brown, and Harvey MacKay who have motivated me and shown me that almost anything I want to accomplish is possible. They will light the way for you, too. Be brave and run from the nay-sayers. They have little to offer except negativity, doubt, and uncertainty.

Thanks to lifelong friends—Fred Miller, Wayne Flewelling, Larry Cohen, Bruce Saber, and Michael Chernoff. They are the people who secure the stars to the sky, and the knowledge that they are just a phone call away is of great comfort to me.

Still not fully comprehending or accepting that he is gone, I wish to remember and thank Richard Higgins. He died too soon to teach me all he knew and too quickly for our friendship to last a lifetime. For the record, I was the only one he allowed to call him "Higgie." I miss you Higgie. Save me a steak.

My sincerest thanks to Jay Cole, a brilliant CFO/COO; Bob Griffin, an extraordinary talent, CEO, and business builder; Andy Karnakas, an inspired and exceptional man, as well as a brilliant intellectual property attorney; and David Steinbach, a gifted recruiter and the hardest working person I know. Further thanks to Joe Kirshenbaum, a corporate executive and lawyer of unmatched intelligence and potential. I thank you all for choosing me as a person worthy of your friendship, conversation, and advice.

Thank you Marty Levin of Gentronics for your generous support of this book and allowing me to interview you. You did this for someone you barely know and for that I will be forever grateful.

My thanks to Kathryn Cottrell, Ph.D. Her insight, ability to examine and consider what she has read, and capacity to make me think are signs of her great and creative mind. Once again, I have a new friend. I would also like to thank Sue Koch for selected help and advice. She is a very smart person.

My heartfelt thanks to all the members of the Westford, Massachusetts, branch of Toastmasters International—the "Westford Expressions." They have welcomed me and fulfilled the promise that is Toastmasters. I urge everyone to join a group in your area. Check out www.toastmasters.org.

It is hard to put into words what Roger Stewart, editorial director at McGraw-Hill, means to me. He took a chance on an unknown, a first-time writer, and gave him the opportunity to expand his potential and ply his craft. I promised not to let him down, and hope I lived up to that promise. Thanks so much, Roger. You are one of the good guys and I hope we can work together again.

I would also like to thank Sachi Guzman and Laurie Stewart who edited this book. They always went the extra mile, did far more than was called for, and made this book much more readable.

I don't remember the day or month, but I do remember the year. It was 1996 when I walked through a bookstore in New York City. And then it was as though I had bumped into a glass door, stunned, but uninjured. That was my reaction to the book-on-tape I saw in front of me. The case was white (the lettering was mostly black, accented with gold) and titled *The Simple Art of Greatness: Building, Managing, and Motivating a Kick-Ass Workforce*. What a great name for a book! (A "kick-ass" workforce? Wow!) On tape, no less.

This tape changed my life in a way that no other business book ever could. It is engaging, fascinating, clear, direct, logical, and so amazingly straightforward that only a man like Mullen could possibly have written it. His examples, his life, his accomplishments, and business practices are astonishing. His voice is so animated and passionate, just hearing him on tape is a great experience. Having said all that, I would like to express my sincerest thanks and appreciation to James X. Mullen, founder and former president of Mullen Advertising, for writing the foreword to this book. Few of us ever get the chance to meet our heroes, and even fewer are still impressed after a closer look. The very idea that he should take the time to do this great favor for a starry-eyed stranger, speaks to the character and generosity of this remarkable man. I will always be grateful for what he has done for me and the impact his book has made on my life. Jim, when last I saw you, your parting words were "Come again." Be careful, I probably will.

Paul Greenberg, author of the book *CRM at the Speed of Light,* is someone I recruited for Live Wire several years ago. He is my developmental editor, confidante, close friend, and one of the smartest people I know. His talent, basic humanity, native intelligence, ability to inspire, people skills, and support have been so very important to this project. To quote from Paul's book, "Writing a book ain't easy." This is quite true and I can say without any doubt, this book would never have happened without Paul's support. Thanks Paul. I owe you.

There is my mother who used to read to me as a child and ignited what will surely be a life-long fascination with and love of books. She is a remarkable person who I will always admire. There is my father who supported my education and taught me the meaning of work. There is my brother, who is not just a brother but a great friend, his wife, Cindy, one of the finest people I know, and their son Dylan Adamsky, a great addition to the family.

Then there is my son Jake, who is a proud member of the United States Navy. I thank him for being my son and teaching me a thing or two about courage, patriotism, and sacrifice. I will always admire the example he set. There is his wife to be, Charllee, and my granddaughter, Jacqueline Marie Adamsky, another great addition to a changing family. There is the last son at home, Nicolai, who let Dad write for three hours every night and only came in to kiss him goodnight. Nick is the most fascinating child I have ever met. He is a great promise of hope and the son every father dreams of having. I love you Nick. Last but not least, there is Wild Bill, who follows his own road and has become more than any of us ever expected. We are all proud of you, Bill.

And finally, there's Judy Cohen. I have known Judy since I was in Mrs. Koch's class in the second grade. That was a very long time ago. Judy and I are both nocturnal by nature and do not like to be spoken to before we have had our morning coffee (especially Judy). When you are up at midnight trying to write a book, there are very few people who wouldn't mind getting a phone call from you. Fortunately for me, Judy is one of them. Being a teacher most of her life, her participation in this project and the review and comments of my manuscript have been a help without which I could never have survived. I will never forget our late night calls and the great insights she added. You were there for me when I cracked my head on the side of the bed wrestling with Gerald, and you are still there for me, fully understanding the difference between chicken chopped liver and liver chopped liver. I thank you for being such a strong and positive influence on my life. You are my friend.

1

Absence of Planning: How Hiring Became Such a Mess

It has been said that failing to plan is planning to fail. Then again, it has also been said that people make plans and God laughs. I am not sure which of these viewpoints is true, but given the odds and my penchant toward the rule of entropy (things go from order to disorder if left to their natural state), I would put my money on planning. You have a greater degree of success if you follow that path.

Planning means many things to many people. For me, planning is the first step toward any endeavor. Look around you. Anything that exists was first planned out in great detail before it was built as a prototype, tested, refined, and then sold. If not, the results would probably have been catastrophic because the "learn as you go" theory can be expensive, frustrating, and very time consuming. The very best companies are deep into the planning stages long before production gets under way.

The prerequisites for building a company are very much the same. The founders need a vision of the kind of organization they are trying to create, long before they assemble the company. Planning applies to small start-up companies as well as medium-sized, struggling companies looking for a change. The importance of planning also applies to the giants that need to reinvent themselves on a regular basis in order to continue to participate, remain competitive, and expand their markets into new and profitable arenas.

The first step in planning should be evaluating, with fresh eyes, what you are trying to accomplish. No preconceived notions are required. If a company is, indeed, nothing more than a collection of its people, then it stands to reason that a "people plan" is where to begin.

The People Plan

I recently had breakfast with Nancy R. Mobley, president of Insight Performance Improvement, Inc. (www.insightperformance.com). Her organization, located in Dedham, Massachusetts, works to define and build human resources systems that will support an organization's growth potential. At the breakfast, Nancy said the following about the importance of a "people plan":

"Can a company grow without the 'people' component? Sure. Can it thrive? Maybe. But only for a short while. Eventually, failure to create and manage a 'people plan' will lead to a disconnect between the vision of the company and the people responsible for implementing the vision. It is essential for you to think through what type of people you need in your organization, what skills are necessary to attain your vision, and what management systems are required to stay proactive. Having a 'people plan' will serve as a guiding light to move management and all employees toward success. Well-thought-out systems that define the goals for recruiting top talent, motivating these individuals to perform as a team, managing and rewarding performance, and proactively developing careers will all lead to a mutual greater good. The end result is enhanced retention and greater productivity, which translate to lower overall cost for the organization."

The first step toward creating this "people plan" is developing a hiring process. This hiring process should aim for simplicity of method and employee retention. If employees are *not* your top priority, you need to revisit your basic premises about what *is* important and re-evaluate. Without employees, there is no company. With that in mind, it is time to look at hiring by utilizing a new and more effective model—a model that will provide a better plan to deal with the rigors of hiring and employee retention—something all companies face.

Seeing Hiring in a New Light

Years ago the job market was a very different place. If you are 40 or older, you know what I mean. Once upon a time, people responded to employment ads in the newspaper. Headhunters were few and far between—and were called "employment agencies." There was no Internet. Computers, less powerful than the one in your briefcase, were the size of Buicks. There were no job fairs, employee referral programs, online recruiting events, or spider bots. A person was hired by mailing in his résumé and cover letter, typed on a typewriter. Most people received simple, polite rejection letters. There are stories about people who received so many rejection letters, they wallpapered them all over their offices. Articles documenting these experiences regularly appeared between the covers of magazines like *Life* and *Look*.

If you were lucky, you received a phone call and an interview. You were elated! This was what you were waiting for, sitting endlessly by the phone. (No answering machines existed. No voicemail. No cell phones.) Even though you weren't guaranteed a job, you were over-joyed just to have an interview. When the day of the interview arrived, you put on your best suit and competed with a lot of others for that same job. You might have gotten an SAI (Sorry After Interview) letter, saying that they really liked you but not enough to give you the posi-tion. If you were *really* lucky, you were put on a short list and called back for a second or third interview. This was almost too much to hope for. An offer usually came in the form of a letter, or a verbal offer was made after the final interview, with a copy to follow in writing. Getting a job was a slow and painful process that could take weeks or longer. If you took another job, there were always others waiting to replace you. No one agonized over your response.

If you are a mid-20s MIT software engineer, expert in JavaScript, HTML, ASP, Perl, C++, NT, and MFC, with five years' work experience, what I just described might seem like a fairy tale. But it isn't. It is all true. Those days, however, are gone. There are no more jobs—there are *positions*. There are no more applicants—there are *candidates*. The can-didate, just like the customer, is king. If you do not recognize this as the simple and basic truth in today's marketplace, you are in trouble. Big trouble. Your life will be one of always being behind the hiring curve and never making your numbers. With this outdated attitude, you will have to be content hiring mediocre candidates, building your company with these individuals. You will live under the terrible pressure to accom-plish the goals of the organization, but will never really live up to the demands that your job requires. Recruiting and closing candidates in today's world is a really tough job. It's like quicksand. If not handled properly, it will swallow your days, nights, weekends, vacations, and health. If this describes any part of your existence, changing the way you see the world of hiring is the very first step in making life better for you and those around you who depend on the services you provide.

The World Today

I do not know you personally, but no matter. Whether you're a first line manager, VP, HR director, recruiter, or CEO, the message is the same: Companies that see the candidate as king do far better than companies that do not. A company's viewpoint drives its actions and its actions speak loudly. Does your company value its employees? What is your company willing to do to retain your employees? The answers will manifest themselves in many ways, and the actions that arise from the answers can really impress the people you interview. Most importantly, your actions can create a great first impression, and few things are more important than that great first impression. Even if the candidates do not make it past the first interview, they will, at the very least, know they spent their time with professionals. This is vital because an organization's reputation is so very important. You always want the word on the street to be positive as it relates to your company.

It is urgent that you philosophically and functionally align yourself and the company with the thinking of your sales and marketing departments. They, like all great organizations, treat their clients with all of the respect, concern, and importance they deserve because clients are the lifeblood of the company and crucial to its survival. Sales departments are proactive. They anticipate client needs even before the clients know the needs exist. Great companies do the same for their employees. In order to be a great company, the company must also be a great employer. Your company—*you*—must anticipate your employees' needs, concerns, and expectations long before they become pressing issues. You must, as Stephen Covey says, in his classic book, *The Seven Habits of Highly Effective People*, work on them in "quadrant-two" time, when the needs are important but not urgent. For example, your VP of sales should be thinking of greater, innovative ways to market product and services in addition to maintaining the happiness and satisfaction of customers. Similarly, your company should be doing the same for your employees, maintaining their happiness and satisfaction, as they are no less important.

Think of your employees as being every bit as important as your customers and you are on your way to a better and smarter reality. You need to continually look for new ways to challenge, motivate, train, reward, and show appreciation for your employees or your competitors will take on that responsibility and take your place. Businesses today, especially in the IT/Technology industry, require these three essentials in order to succeed and remain competitive:

- ▶ Great customers

- ▶ Great partners

- ▶ Great employees

Treat any of them shabbily and each could very well join the competition, taking contacts, relationships, intellectual property, bad feelings, and fellow employees with them. There are very few résumés today being submitted in any way other than by email, especially in the world of IT professionals and technologists. (I can't remember the last time I received a résumé by snail mail.) And response time to these résumés is critical. When a potential candidate cruises the Web looking for a job, she can easily respond to multiple postings in a very short time—all it takes is a few mouse clicks. How quickly will your staff respond? Wait until after tomorrow's lunch and you may find that the candidate already has four other interviews and is continuing to get calls from your competition. You now have a serious problem. Your competition is anyone who wants to take your employees, your customers, your market share, and then builds a Burger King where your company used to be. (They don't say business is half war and half sport for nothing. On some days it is *all* war.) In the battle to find and hire the best employees, speed is so important that you must run as fast as possible just to stay competitive. Simply stated, there are the quick and there are the dead. It is so important to forward incoming résumés to the appropriate hiring managers before the competition has a chance to do the same. This means first thing in the morning. Candidates are so impressed when they get a call or email response immediately because it makes them feel important and acknowledged. It also speaks volumes about the company.

Change Starts at Senior Management's Door

In order to look at hiring in a new light, senior management must be committed to the philosophy that hiring the right employees is critical to the overall success of an organization. Furthermore, senior management must work closely with their hiring managers to develop this commitment at all levels of the organization. There is no such thing as an unimportant hire because any hire affects an organization in one way or another. It should be the priority of the executive team to communicate the importance of hiring the right people as early on in the development of the company as possible. Procrastination leads to lost opportunity and "things that might have been." The time to make this commitment to excellence is now. Otherwise, all that follows will be hollow, half-hearted acts practiced by those who do not really believe in the cause. In the end, they will ultimately fall back to their old ways.

In addition, every position profile should include a statement specifying that the employee is responsible for doing whatever he or she can to promote the company's growth curve. I have seen too many managers grumble about having to interview endless candidates, but that *is* part of their responsibility. If you are a manager who is fortunate enough to be part of an organization that is growing, interviewing simply comes with the territory. If you are a manager who has open positions, it is in your best interest to interview aggressively and fill these positions quickly. Doing so will allow you the time to get on with the business of adding value to your organization by meeting departmental objectives, mentoring your direct reports, and leading by example.

The alternative is running around like a crazy person, trying to do your job as well as the jobs of three other people. Very unproductive! Try to see interviewing as an opportunity—the chance to hire people who will support your success, make your life less stressful, and help you to groom a capable "partner" who can share your responsibilities and move forward within the organization. This concept is important because many managers are often quietly passed over for promotion because senior management feels there is no one in the department who can take the current manager's place. If you think that being the only person who can do a job is a good thing, think again. Unless you want to be in the same position for 90 years, don't let this happen to you. Manage your career within the organization because if you don't manage your own career, the organization will manage it for you. And that is the last thing you want.

....

Set the tone for your group by being happy, enthusiastic, and positive about interviewing. In the long run, this will serve you best.

Remember, IT professionals can go out and get multiple offers far easier than you can interview enough people to make multiple hires. For this reason alone, I urge you to make the commitment to hiring effectively a top priority. You will see results and be pleased with the positive changes that take place within your organization.

Develop a Hiring Process

If the space allotted to the hiring process appears to be excessive compared to the space devoted to other subjects in this chapter, it is by design. The careful development, appropriate modification, and consistent utilization of the interviewing and hiring infrastructure are extremely important. These aspects are very often the measure of how effective the entire candidate selection, interviewing, decision-making, and hiring process is within your organization. If you have no consistent, effective hiring system, filling just a few positions ineffectively can be a catastrophe. I have seen companies operate with no hiring process in place and the results can be disastrous. On one occasion, an offer was made to two applicants for only one available position. To make matters worse, the two applicants, both having received offers, resigned from their current positions to take the new position. But, that's not all! One candidate was offered ten thousand dollars more than the other candidate! It turns out, there was no one person to blame because there was no hiring process for anyone to follow in the first place. Fortunately, a creative solution was found—a new position was created for the more experienced candidate, and the original open position was given to the less experienced applicant. Had some creative employment engineering not been readily available, this situation would have been disastrous. More often than not, this situation *would* have resulted in disaster.

Recently, I was given the task of doubling the size of a technology company, just outside of Boston, in less than seven months. It went off without a hitch because the infrastructure we put in place was simple and bulletproof, even at a breakneck speed. This is the goal you need to set for your company because the alternative will be chaos, unfilled positions, angry hiring managers, and irate candidates.

Developing an interviewing and hiring infrastructure can be as simple or as complicated as you wish to make it. The process should be designed to be as straightforward as possible. Naturally, the larger and more complex the organization, the more difficult this task can be. But, simplicity is still the target. Keep in mind that, for the candidate, the company will be judged by how you handle the hiring process. Candidates should not fall through the cracks, should be communicated with in an accurate and timely manner, and should not be left in the dark about when the next step will take place and what the next step will be.

The following suggested process is generic. It may not work for some organizations but it is a good place to start. Sensible modifications should be made in order to make the plan fit your company's specific needs and requirements. This is a "living" document that needs to be revisited on a regular basis and modified to meet current staffing and logistical conditions.

Getting Started

The hiring manager completes the Requisition for Personnel section of a Requisition/HR Action Form. (The Requisition for Personnel section triggers the recruiting process; the HR Action Form section acts as the final okay for a new candidate hire.)

The signatures of the following people are required on the Personnel/ HR Action Form:

▶ The hiring manager

▶ The next level manager

▶ The director of HR

Next, a recruiter is assigned to move the process forward.

The Recruiter Hunts and Gathers

The search process begins when the recruiter determines the most effective and cost-efficient method to fill the position(s).

All résumés should be sent to the recruiter for screening and date stamping to avoid double agency fees. (Agencies will be discussed in greater detail in Chapter 2.) Briefly, agencies are third-party organizations that supply companies with candidates. Agencies can be contingent: They are paid only if the candidate is hired. Retained agencies are paid one-third of the total fee up front and will keep the one-third even if no candidate is placed. Contingency agencies are the most common type of agency, and retained agencies are usually for more senior-level positions. The purpose of date stamping agency résumés is to prevent more than one agency from submitting the same candidate, and in turn, prevents you from getting in the middle of an agency war for the fee. If you date stamp all agency résumés as they arrive, the agency that first submitted the résumé will receive the fee if the candidate is hired. Date stamping should include the date *and* time of arrival. I have seen the same résumé come in the door three times from three different agencies in one day.

In these instances, noting the *time* the résumé is received is critical. I personally like to receive résumés by email so I can immediately access them if ever a conflict arises. In this way, I can determine which agency sent the résumé first and it is a good way to avoid double fees, agency wars, and other forms of unpleasantness.

The recruiter must take responsibility for the following actions:

1. Screen and select primary candidates and send the résumés to the hiring manager. The recruiter should use his or her own judgment in choosing the most appropriate candidates to interview. If in doubt, the recruiter should screen the candidates by phone, and can ask a preselected series of questions related to the position to be filled. The questions should be supplied by the hiring manager.

2. Send the screened candidates' résumés to the hiring manager for review. The hiring manager can choose to interview each candidate (or not). If the hiring manager is unsure of candidates, he or she can also screen them by phone. (You don't want to pass up a good candidate who might not have a polished résumé.)

3. Log résumés on an applicant tracking log. The log data can later be used to determine which recruitment methods are most effective. Furthermore, the information on the applicant tracking log will help you track the interview process and progress of each candidate.

The Hiring Manager Makes Some Decisions

The hiring manager makes recruitment a priority by reviewing résumés and returning them to the recruiter within 48 hours. The following should be indicated on the top of each résumé for action to be taken by the recruiter:

Interest/phone screen by manager This means that the hiring manager has enough interest to conduct a phone screen of the candidate but not enough interest to bring the candidate in for a face-to-face interview.

Interest/bring in for interview This means that the hiring manager has enough interest to bring the candidate in for a face-to-face interview.

No Interest/hold for other positions This means that the hiring manager likes the candidate for other possible positions but does not feel that the candidate meets the specifications of the position for which the candidate originally applied.

The hiring manager must also create a list of people who will be on the interviewing team and supply the list to the hiring manager's administrator who will be handling all of the important details. (The administrator is the person who handles the minutiae and works very hard and seldom gets credit.)

Setting Up the Interviews

The recruiter should work with the hiring manager's administrator to arrange the appropriate schedule of interviews, paying close attention to names, dates, and times. All candidates should be emailed the directions to the interview site, the phone number of the hiring manager, and the link to the website of the organization.

The Interviews

Interviewing will be covered in greater detail in Chapter 3. However, please make note of the following essentials for you to think about now:

Be prepared Greet the candidates enthusiastically and let them know you were expecting them. Offer coffee or some other beverage and welcome them to the company. Confusion and lack of preparedness is not a great way to kick off the interview process and impress the candidate in a positive way.

Do not make the candidate wait The first interviewer should be notified as soon as the candidate arrives. The candidate should not have to wait for more than five minutes.

The interview is *not* the time to be reading the candidate's résumé for the first time Thoroughly read the candidate's résumé. Twice. Not 60 seconds before the candidate arrives. You cannot conduct a good interview if you are not prepared, and the candidate will know when you are not prepared.

Provide the candidate with an interviewing schedule The candidate is in unfamiliar territory. Recognize this, and give the candidate an interviewing schedule with the names of all the interviewers, their positions, and the proposed timeframe for each interview. You will look more prepared than 90 percent of the companies you are competing against. Make every effort to keep on schedule and respect the candidate's time.

Conduct a mini-tour of your organization   Attempt to make the candidate feel at home with a quick tour of the company or the department in which he or she might be working. Make an introduction or two. This may help to put the candidate at ease, and a relaxed candidate interviews better.

End the interview by thanking the candidate   Very few people do this, but it is absolutely necessary. The candidate most likely did a lot of work to prepare for the interview, and has given up a good portion of the day to meet you. Thanking the candidate for his or her time is the very least you can do.

AFTER THE FIRST INTERVIEW

1. The recruiter should collect feedback from all the hiring managers within 24 hours of the first interview. The best way to do this is to gather all interviewers in a room and talk about their reactions to the candidate. Find out if they think another interview is warranted.

2. The recruiter should get back to each candidate with news that the group is interested in having the candidate return for a second interview or have the administrator send out an SAI letter. (The SAI or "Sorry After Interview" letter indicates that the candidate has not been selected for a second interview and is not being considered for the position.)

AFTER THE SECOND INTERVIEW

1. The recruiter should collect feedback within 24 hours of the second interview in same manner stated above.

2. The recruiter should get back to the candidate, informing him or her of a second interview, or have the administrator send out an SAI letter in same manner stated above.

3. The recruiter secures candidate references for a reference check if an offer is to be made. References should be checked only if

there is a genuine interest in hiring a candidate. There should be two references: one from a previous supervisor and one from a peer. If the job being offered is a technical sales position, one reference should be from a person who was a customer of the candidate.

When checking references, the hiring manager should check one, and the recruiter should check one. Reference notes should be kept in writing and placed in the candidate's folder. It is beneficial for the hiring manager to check at least one of the references in order to get a good feel for the candidate's strengths and weaknesses first hand.

The Offer

If the offer is within the set salary range, the recruiter is told to prepare the offer letter for mailing. The offer is dependent on whether the references were satisfactory. A tip! Always check with the hiring manager before the offer is actually mailed. I have seen managers change their minds at the last minute for every known reason, so always confirm the final decision.

If the offer is not within the set salary range, written approval (by email or by signature on the original requisition) must come from both the director of HR and the hiring manager. This is a good way to ensure that no one has gone outside of the compensation guidelines without permission. (People have short memories. An approval given at the spur of the moment might not be remembered six months later.)

An offer can be made by phone by the hiring manager or a designee. If the candidate accepts by phone, the manager can secure a start date at that time. Very often, the candidate will accept a phone offer pending review of the written offer. This is perfectly normal, as candidates often feel more secure with a written offer to review.

When a written offer is sent, a copy of the letter should be kept with the recruiter. All offer letters should be sent by overnight mail, or at the very least, by priority mail. There is always bit of pomp and circumstance surrounding a job offer, and the manner in which you send it should reflect its importance. Written offers should not be open-ended. It is not unreasonable to ask the candidate to sign and return the letter within five to seven business days. Be advised that the candidate might be entertaining other offers, traveling, or doing any of a number of things that might slow down the response time by a day or two. However, be on the lookout for people who are stalling. Common sense dictates that it makes no sense to lose a candidate because he or she is a few days late in returning the offer letter. If a candidate needs an inordinate amount of time to make a decision, try to determine what the problem is and act accordingly. In one case I was involved with, I discovered that a candidate wanted to get a number of offers before making a decision. I told the candidate to take all of the time she needed to shop around, and if she was still interested in the position, and it was still open, we would talk again. She came back in less than four weeks and asked for the offer. It was made and she accepted in less than three days.

All accepted offers should be communicated through the recruiter. At that time, the recruiter should communicate the acceptance or rejection to human resources as well as to the hiring manager. Remember that a returned offer letter with no signature or agreed starting date is worthless.

Getting Onboard

When the signed offer letter has been returned by the candidate, it is time to prepare for the arrival of your new employee. First, notify all departments and staff who will be involved in the preparation. Make sure all equipment, supplies, and tools needed to accomplish his or her duties are ready and available (e.g., a phone, desk, computer, email account, Internet access, etc.). If for any reason all preparations have not been completed before your employee's first day of work, he or she should be made to feel that everything possible was done to get things in order. Provide information as to when all arrangements are expected to be completed.

Never underestimate the importance of the new employee's first day at your company. If "Lisa" feels you were not ready for her arrival, or that her needs weren't taken seriously, she will never forget her first day. I have done exit interviews with employees who were able to tell me about the horrors of their first day on the job as if it were yesterday. In some cases, they arrived for their first day of work and did not even have a desk. One employee told me that the company did not even have his start date correctly recorded. He arrived and no one knew who he was. Twenty years later, the anger was still there. Do not let this happen to any of your new employees. If you don't think you will be properly ready for your employee's first day, use your judgment and call the candidate to have him start a day or two later than originally planned (with full compensation, of course). This is better than to have him come in to an organization that appears disorganized and uncaring. You need to make him feel as though he made the right decision by joining your company. You do this not by your words but by your actions. Assign someone to be responsible to see that everything is being prepared correctly for the new hire's arrival.

The Orientation

The new hire orientation is very important. It should, depending on the size of your company, be held at 9:00 A.M. every Monday morning, if at all possible. At that time, new employees will complete the new hire paperwork and will receive an employee handbook (more on this later), a copy of the company mission statement, operating principles, and benefits information. It is important that HR be responsible for ensuring that the newly hired employee has all necessary paperwork completed and it be sent to the proper payroll and benefits personnel to ensure accurate insurance coverage and correctly delivered compensation. No employee wants to hear that the first paycheck will be two weeks late because someone made a mistake with the paperwork. Remember, the employee is looking for signs that he made the right decision by joining your company. Do not give reason to doubt this decision at such a critical time. Get your administrative process right and stick to it. Lastly, depending on the level of the new employee, he or she should be introduced to appropriate employees and departments.

Wrapping Up the Hiring Process

From outside the organization, the hiring process should be seamless and invisible. All the candidate is interested in is whether he or she is moving on to the next step or is being dropped from further consideration. Make sure that all candidates brought in for interviews are communicated with as quickly as possible regarding what the next step will be. (If you tell a candidate that you are going to do something, do it!) After the interview, there is only one of three possibilities:

▶ The candidate continues to the next phase of the interview process.

▶ The candidate is held for consideration against other candidates. Make this hold a very short one. Good candidates have better things to do than wait around for you to make a decision.

▶ The candidate does not continue to the next phase of the process because management has decided that the candidate will not be receiving an offer.

In *any* case, the candidate should have the decision communicated to him or her as soon as possible. Candidates who have to wait too long to receive information are not happy people. This dissatisfaction reflects badly on your organization and is bad PR. You don't want former candidates going around speaking ill of your company.

Easy access to your candidates' status is important. People inside the organization should be able to find out where the candidate is in the hiring process at any time.

Constant communication with the candidate is important. Just as you are juggling candidates, candidates are juggling offers from various companies. Communicate with each candidate clearly, honestly, and effectively. Despite the final outcome, the candidate will have respect for you and your organization.

Be a Class Act: Respond to All Candidates

Most companies do not respond to every candidate who sends in a résumé. They usually respond only to the candidates they are interested in interviewing. There are various schools of thought regarding whether to respond to every résumé because of the sheer volume that might be received as a result of hiring events such as job fairs or advertisements. Although it is not the end of the world if you do not respond to everyone, sending out postcards to those who have taken the trouble to send résumés makes you look classier than those who simply do nothing. Send a postcard to candidates who responded by standard mail and send an automated email response to those who contacted you by email. Short and to the point, the correspondence should say something like the following:

We at HR Innovators received your résumé and thank you for your interest in our company. We review all résumés and will be in touch if your qualifications meet our current needs. We wish you the very best of luck in your job search.

—Corinne Adamsky

SAI Letters

It is important to send out a "Sorry After Interview" letter if a candidate has been phone screened or interviewed, and you have decided not to move forward in pursuing the candidate. The letter should be mailed soon after you have made this decision, and it should be short, clear, and to the point. The purpose of this letter is to communicate your decision, and is not designed to be an apology. A sample SAI letter is shown here.

Dear Mr. Smith:

On behalf of the staff and management of HR Innovators, I would like to thank you for taking the time to meet with us. Your skills and experience are impressive, but at this time, we are looking for candidates whose backgrounds more closely align with our specific needs. Thank you for your interest and we wish you well in your job search.

Best regards,

Corinne Adamsky

The Importance of Making a Phone Call

In some cases, candidates will come in for several interviews, meet with many different managers and peers, and spend a good deal of time at the company. Once a final decision has been made and a job offer given and accepted, it is best to acknowledge the time and efforts of each candidate by contacting the finalists by phone. (Never do this before you receive a signed offer letter! For more on this, read Chapter 5.) Let the final candidates know they did extraordinarily well in their series of interviews, but another candidate has been chosen. From personal experience, I know this is not an easy call to make—I do not like making them myself, and it never seems to get much easier. The call should be short, sincere, and pleasant. However, it should not be an apology or a long conversation to explain where the candidate fell short. It is best to say that the final candidate had more experience in some of the specific areas that the organization requires at this time. If well executed, a call makes the candidate feel better than the standard SAI letter. You never know whether you will run into the candidate again, so it is best to be remembered with kindness. The important thing here is that you never want to leave the candidate hanging.

One final thought on candidate communication: In all but the rarest, delicate, or political situations, it is not required or expected that you communicate directly with a candidate who is represented by an agency. This is one of the advantages of third-party organizations; they act as the conduit for all communication.

Selling the Hiring Process

Selling the hiring process to the right people within your organization is the key to success. You don't necessarily get people to buy into an idea simply by being the CEO and issuing an executive order. Many captains of industry may disagree with me, but I have seen CEOs and company presidents issue an order for all to follow, then watch employees say "yes," and go right back to business as usual two days later. This is an aspect of company culture that bears mentioning. The CEO might be "the big cheese," but processes are really only followed when people see how the processes will benefit them. Employees partner up with you because they see that it is in their best interest to do so and it will somehow make their jobs easier. If you think they will follow processes because you issued an executive order, you might very well be surprised. Remember, no buy in from the staff, at all levels, and the hiring process becomes a nonentity, loses its intended effectiveness, and will result in chaos.

Selling the hiring process requires no more than reviewing it with the hiring managers and those who interview on a regular basis. It also involves thanking them for work well done and asking them what you can do to make the process easier, more efficient, and more effective. If you take people's suggestions and incorporate them into the process, they will feel an ownership of the plan. You will be far more likely to receive the support you are looking for. Occasional monitoring of the hiring process is an important aspect of keeping it current and relevant to your organization's changing needs. A hiring process that worked well last year might not work well a year later.

At times, people will not follow the process that has been put in place. Despite the temptation, this need not be punishable by death. Well-meaning people work hard, do the best they can, and still slip. When I run across these situations, I make a point of telling the offending person how much I appreciate how hard he or she tries to follow the process. Let your people know that if they get overloaded, you will give them assistance or assign another person to the task. At one point, I managed to get my hands on 25 gift certificates to the food court. I gave them out very judiciously—not to people who were wonderful about following the system, but to those who struggled to follow the system. The difference this made in their attitudes and performance was remarkable. Pats on the back for a job well done are a good idea and far more effective than berating someone for the occasional oversight. If you use the carrot wisely, the stick is rarely necessary. If you remember the importance of selling the process as a time saver that will also make things easier and less painful, you will probably do well and achieve the results you are looking for.

Developing a Hiring Strategy

Now that you have a solid hiring process, you must determine who it is that your organization needs. Recruiting is difficult without a well-thought-out hiring strategy, and part of that strategy is knowing what your needs are and what types of people you want to hire. Because the hiring plan is a strategic component of the overall hiring process, decisions must be made at the senior-most levels of the organization. A solid hiring plan includes input from anyone at the VP level who is involved in hiring because, often, the recruiting dollars come out of the departments' budgets. The hiring strategy should also have the blessing of the CFO who will be involved as an internal business partner to provide input and support to the hiring managers. All good hiring plans should include the following:

- ▶ A breakdown, by department, of which positions need to be filled

- ▶ A set of priorities for filling these positions, either cascading—as soon as the first position is filled then the next one falls into the top priority slot—or projected quarterly—positions prioritized solely by timeframe.

I cannot stress the importance of developing a hiring strategy strongly enough. Just as a hiring process is necessary to make the recruiting machine run smoothly, the hiring strategy is equally necessary to ensure everyone is on the same page regarding which positions should be filled and the order in which they are to be filled. (It is also important to communicate the hiring strategy to the entire organization.)

Candidates are also affected by the organized and proper implementation of the strategy. If they happen to ask what positions you will be filling over the next few months, you and your company will look well organized and secure if you can answer the question. Simply shrugging your shoulders will give the impression that your organization does not have it all together. I once worked with an HR director who did not believe in the importance of communicating the strategy and getting full support from the staff. He believed that this all-important strategy should be shared on a need-to-know basis. Confusion reigned supreme as no one was really sure who was to be hired and in what order. That company is gone now and this HR director is currently parking cars in southern New Jersey for a living. I am not sure of the exact location as it is on a need-to-know basis!

Compensation: More than Just a Number

It is impossible to hire and retain employees if you are completely in the dark about the more important aspects of compensation. I have always admired compensation experts. They seem to be part CFO, part statistician, and part family therapist, with a dash of business-based human resources guru thrown in for good measure. They have endless data, tend to be very fastidious, and highly opinionated. Good compensation experts keep informed about the current needs within the organization. They are also constantly on the lookout for the latest theories and practices that arise in the field of compensation. Research into new and different compensation models is always being conducted to develop more creative ways to motivate employees. However, all compensation experts seem to agree on the two theories described in the following sections.

Compensation Drives Performance

Money most often drives people's actions, and compensation programs are built around delivering money. Remember that more often than not, when it comes down to offer time, the "price" as reflected in the total compensation package becomes very important to the candidate.

The compensation your organization offers is indicative of how an employee is valued by your organization. The higher the level of compensation, the greater the perceived value of the employee. This is a fact of corporate life. There is no way you can argue that a $90,000 a year employee is valued less by an organization than a $50,000 a year employee. This is a fact of economic reality, corporate perception, and the laws of market value. However, to a candidate, "how much" is often as important as "how," especially when there is an element of variable compensation (i.e., compensation received in addition to base pay that varies based on the performance of the employee, team, or company). Thomas B. Wilson, a national authority on reward systems (see www.wilsongroup.com), offers this opinion: "Be careful what you measure and reward; you will surely get more of it."

So, the best compensation systems go beyond just delivering money to people. They also influence the actions of people. And, according to Wilson, the best compensation plans "encourage and reinforce those actions that make the company more successful."

The Right Compensation Plan Is Essential

One thing that must be considered is the importance of providing the new employee with the right compensation plan. Providing an inappropriate compensation plan will greatly diminish the potential success of that employee. A bad incentive plan could reward and reinforce the wrong behavior. Many managers have spoken to me about times when candidates were not doing what they were supposed to be doing. In these situations, the first thing I ask is how the candidate is compensated and what functions are supposed to be performed. The candidates are probably responding to what they think their manager expected.

If compensation and the job's function are not in alignment, there will be problems. Not always, but very often, the problems can be traced to compensation, the measures of performance, or both. For example, if you compensate a technical sales executive with a straight base salary and no incentive compensation, there is little incentive for him or her to go to work in the morning because the earnings will be the same whether he or she sells. There are many examples of problems caused by not developing the right plan for the position being filled.

The most common types of compensation are as follows:

▶ Base salary/wage compensation that is paid out to the employee with a check on a regular basis, with all of the appropriate taxes deducted (a weekly or bimonthly paycheck).

▶ Incentive compensation that is paid out for meeting specific expectations that were previously established. It can be a percent of the value created (revenues, profits, etc.) or a dollar amount that relates to the value of what was produced. Incentive compensation is a standard in the executive and sales worlds, but it is now appearing in compensation programs of employees other than just those working in sales (e.g., customer service, marketing, and operations).

▶ Bonuses, which are similar to incentive compensation, but sometimes not as tightly defined, are payouts tied to the achievement of an objective, goal, or critical milestone. For example, a bonus can be paid out if a development team reaches a milestone before a predetermined date. Another type of bonus is a sign-on bonus. It is a one-time bonus for accepting a position, usually paid in two installments: one paid 30 days after the employee starts and one paid 60 days after. Different companies have different policies regarding the sign-on bonus, but it should not be paid out all at once on the date of hire. Doing so is a great risk to the company. Sign-on bonuses are paid instead of providing the new hire with a higher base salary because it is a one-time payment that does not increase overhead or risk salary equity among current employees.

▶ Stock options can be awarded to employees as an incentive to join the company as a tradeoff for lower cash compensation. Stock options can also be a standard part of the compensation program that is awarded to selected individuals on an annual basis. Some companies offer stock options to everyone. This type of compensation can be very complex, but to generalize, the more valuable you are to the company, the more stock options you will be given. They are awarded by a predetermined plan that is adopted by the company, but the sooner you join the company, the more options there are to give out. Plus, the more the company grows and achieves market leadership, the greater will be the value of the stock options. The number of options you get is based on personal contributions, and the value of the options is based on the company's value in the marketplace.

A word of advice on compensation: *simplicity*. Jim Mullen, founder of Mullen Advertising, says in *The Simple Art of Greatness*, "The world is made up of simplifiers and complexifiers. Beware the complexifiers." I have seen compensation plans that are so complicated I can hardly understand them. Compensation plans should be, at all levels and for all positions, as simple as they can be crafted. Wilson also makes a key point by saying, "All compensation plans need to be simple to understand and manage, but not simplistic" (because simplistic programs will not encourage desired results).

Another very important component to consider regarding compensation is the concept of equitable salary. I suggest developing a matrix that can be used to plot the salaries of people within the same job classification. This matrix should consist of two elements, described in the following sections.

Data from Outside the Organization

Data from outside your organization can come from compensation-related websites like www.salaryticker.com. They provide recruiting firms and employers with compensation information on the "going-rate"—the salary, hiring bonus, incentive targets, and other key information. This new and rapidly growing site is the first to provide credible information on hiring rates. The data can also come from organizations that collect compensation data from employers and sell this data to those who wish to see where they stand in comparison to other organizations that are in the same industry. You can locate these companies on the Web if you are inclined to pay to participate. You can use them to inform yourself about what the rest of the world is doing when it comes to specific compensation issues. This information may or may not affect your decision about where to place a candidate within your corporate compensation range, but having the knowledge up front will help you know where you and your candidate stand. If data is needed for periodic references, websites like www.salaryticker.com and others that offer standard survey information on a transaction basis are often the most cost effective.

Data from Inside the Organization

It is essential that you consider the compensation data within your organization—the salaries of your employees in the same job classification. Here is an example why: If all of your network administrators are earning $55,000 and you hire someone with the same skill sets at $70,000, you risk creating major conflicts around fairness and perceived "worth" in the middle of your company. You might think that employee compensation is confidential. Surprisingly, this is not true. Most people know what others are making because people talk. It is part of the work culture. Even though everyone has a right to compensation privacy, the information manages to get around anyway. According to a former mentor, internal compensation equity has been achieved if, after having gathered all of your employees in a room and posted everyone's salaries on a white board, most people in the group feel okay with the numbers. This of course is not an easy thing to accomplish.

If you are one of the fortunate ones just starting a company, you are at an advantage because you are starting with a clean slate. If you are part of a well-established organization, you most likely already have compensation programs in place with a series of guidelines you follow as closely as possible. Regardless of the type of organization, there are three very important factors to consider:

- ▶ First, you must develop an in-depth knowledge of your industry's pay trends and practices (i.e., know how others are being paid).

- ▶ Second, you need to know what people are being paid within your industry at all levels (i.e., know how much others in related jobs are being paid).

- ▶ Third, you need to understand what actions the compensation plans are encouraging and rewarding. Do these actions fit your business strategy and the job you want the person to do? Are the amount and structure of the deal sufficiently competitive for you to attract the talent you want? Will it help you retain the talent you need?

Few positions should be compensated by base salary alone in order to motivate a person to work more effectively. Incentives can create a degree of excitement and encourage people to do their jobs better. Incentives do not cost the organization more because the payout should be generated from the savings created by people being more effective, creative, and efficient at what they do. Even small incentives can result in significant savings for the organization by increasing customer focus and efficiency, and decreasing cost. In the end, it will put more money in the pocket of the employee *and* the organization, creating a win-win situation.

Get It Right the First Time!

Of all of the rules regarding compensation, this one takes precedence over all others.

In the mad rush to hire people, money is thrown at situations, resulting in problems for both the company and the candidate. The company sets up deals that may be counterproductive to the strategy or performance requirements; the candidate enters the company with unrealistic expectations of future compensation. An appropriate and well-thought-out compensation program is essential to the long-term effectiveness of the employee and the success of the organization.

If you fail to compensate employees correctly and appropriately, you could end up wondering why your new employee is spending so much time doing things that have very little to do with what you want him or her to be doing. I have seen sales executives with incentive plans that reflect IT-type compensation plans, delivery dates, and "discretionary" elements; software engineers with incentive plans that are more appropriate for administrators; and senior executives with only a base salary and little promise for more in the future—no incentives, no bonuses, no options. These problems tend to magnify themselves as a company grows. Keep in mind that it is always better to set up the right compensation program in the beginning than to try to fix problems later. It is very difficult and awkward to alter compensation programs once an organization is established, but if it needs to be done, try to get it right the second time.

People Are Touchy About Money—Don't Mess with a Compensation Plan

The subject of money is a very sensitive and emotional one. Making adjustments to established compensation programs is extremely disturbing to people and almost always causes deterioration in trust and performance until the issues are resolved. Many complain more about the process than they do about the "new deal."

Like it or not, change is difficult for people to deal with and very often there is an underlying distrust of senior management. It is important that if you change the incentive or overall structure of the compensation package that you do not discourage a new employee by cutting salary or presenting a new package that does not at least equal the earning potential of the original compensation plan. If the individual can see that a new program is clear, linked to factors he or she can control and influence, and is achievable, then change may not be seen as negative. Through his extensive research and consulting experience, Wilson has discovered how plans that become more meaningful to employees actually turn out to provide them with a better sense of opportunity and encourage greater commitment and motivation.

But the process of developing the revisions is often as important as the resulting plan—it reflects the real values of the company.

Major changes to compensation that do not improve the program is one of the main reasons people consider looking for other employment opportunities. This kind of turnover will have a direct impact on an organization's stability. I cannot emphasize the importance of getting it right the first time. Plan each package carefully and be sure the candidate understands his or her compensation plan, how it is paid out, and is satisfied with the deal.

Dealing with compensation issues is one of the most delicate aspects of the entire hiring process and can take months of hard work. Your goal is to make an offer that will be viewed as fair and acceptable. You have to weigh all of the data, including the candidate's current salary, and balance it with the needs of your organization and your organization's need for this candidate. It is not easy to get full agreement among all parties. I recall a close friend and mentor who would discuss offers with me in his office. He liked to pull out all of his salary surveys, draw pictures, plot graphs and spreadsheets, and go to the Internet to come up with the right number to offer a candidate. This is all well and good, but you don't want the candidate to die of old age waiting for the right number. My way was to see what the candidate was making, do a benefits comparison, look at the candidate's commute time, and ask what it will take to make him join the organization. Then I came up with a number. One kind of approach is to base the offer on the numbers, trends, and practices, and the other is to base it on what is meaningful to the individual and the organization.

Despite anything anyone might say, you never really know what is in a candidate's head regarding compensation until the end when discussions about compensation intensify. If a candidate happens to read an article in the *Wall Street Journal* on Sunday that says technology compensation has jumped an average of 13 percent over the last year, you are going to hear about it from your candidate. Compensation issues often lead the list of subjects needing last-minute negotiations.

In almost all cases, the potential employee is looking for the most he or she can get in terms of a starting base salary. Incentives and stock options are often discounted because they are based on a desired, but perhaps not achievable, future. Stock options are not as appealing as they were just a few years ago because of the tremendous volatility of the security markets. However, hiring managers still sometimes prefer to pay the least for what he or she can get. This can cause a huge rift between the candidate and the organization that can last months into employment. You must realize that money is often a symbolic reflection of a person's sense of self-worth or ego. I have seen deals fall apart at the last minute over compensation that equals the cost of a sandwich. I have also seen parties that are initially far apart on the issues pull together to form a deal by utilizing a dizzying array of arrangements because both parties were invested in and committed to making it work. When developing an offer, it is important to realize that fairness, opportunity for advancement, and internal equity are critical issues to be considered. Let's examine these issues one at a time.

Candidates Must Feel Good About the Deal

Fairness can have many meanings. In the world of compensation, fairness is the feeling that both parties have come to a reasonable agreement and feel good about the outcome. This final employment agreement sets the tone for the entire working relationship. You never want candidates to enter an employment agreement thinking they were taken advantage of because they will carry the resentment with them for the entire time they are with your company. (What type of work do you think these employees will perform and provide with that level of resentment?)

Candidates Must Understand the Value of the Entire Package

Help the candidate understand that the starting base salary is the least amount of money he or she will ever make within your organization. It is important to help the candidate see the entire picture—how she plays an important role in the success of the organization. Having candidates understand the long-term benefits of joining the company is key. Here are some areas to focus on:

- ► The vision the organization has for them and their role within the organization

- ► The opportunities that exist for advancement

- ► Annual bonuses

- ► Corporate benefits

- ► Corporate culture

- ► Anything else that the candidates may value: Location, a larger office, free refreshments or meals, paid memberships to organizations, discounts on entertainment, etc.

The base salary is only a part of the entire picture and it is your responsibility to lead the candidate to see all of the benefits of what you are offering.

Let Good Judgment Be Your Guide

Internal equity is very important within an organization. How would you feel if one of your peers were earning 40 percent more than you, yet has the same level of experience and is doing the same job? This is a scenario you should avoid. In rare cases, employment inequities can be acceptable. For example, an employee in a start-up company might be making considerably less in cash compensation than a new hire with the same experience, but because the first employee was hired early on in the company's development, that person might have considerably more stock options than the new hire. Before you make an offer, review your internal and external data. If the candidate you want to hire is making too much money in his current job to fit into the your existing internal equity structure, there are a number of things you can do. This will be discussed in detail in Chapter 5.

Beyond the simple numbers, there is something else to think about. Your organization must determine where it wants to place itself within the compensation range for all positions. For example, should the salaries be situated at the lower end of the salary scale when compared with the competition? The middle? The upper end of the spectrum? This is not an easy decision to make, and what your organization decides will have significant implications on the types of people you hire, the type of products you produce, your pricing strategy, your niche in the marketplace, how you are perceived by those within your industry, and a host of other variables. Many of my clients choose to be 20 percent above or below the median because this gives them a good deal of latitude to adjust for market conditions and changes in philosophy and positioning.

Develop a Simple Employee Handbook

Every company should have an employee handbook that is a straightforward guideline outlining the company's mission statement, operating principles, employee benefits, company policies and procedures, holiday schedule, etc. Many organizations put everything in the employee handbook, including the kitchen sink, because they want to protect themselves from lawsuits or protect against employees trying to beat the system. This is logical on the surface, but tends to work in reverse. The deeper and more complex the handbook, the more loopholes and interpretations there are. Once again, the employee handbook should be simple and straightforward. It is best to outsource the development of the handbook to those who specialize in doing them. No sense in reinventing the wheel if you don't have to. Having a competent employment lawyer review it from a legal standpoint is also a very good idea.

Benefits

Benefits are second only to compensation in terms of the information people examine and care about most. Benefits can make up as much as 30 percent of some compensation packages, but usually fall within the range of 22 to 28 percent in most organizations. In general, employees who are right out of college are happy enough to get into the workforce and have some money for a change. They usually do not look at benefits as closely as those who have a family. As people mature, medical, dental, and vision benefits; 401(k); long- and short-term disability; and sick days all become more attractive and important.

When benefits are discussed (usually at the second interview), present the candidate with what is called a "benefits at a glance" summary (Figure 1-1). It is simply a one-page overview of the company benefits that can be reviewed at the candidate's leisure.

What Kind of Benefits?

Benefits, like compensation, are not just a practical nuts and bolts issue. What kind of benefits do you want to offer? How much? How little? As a result, benefits selection is something that needs to be addressed, planned out, and evaluated by senior management. Do you want to offer more benefits or fewer benefits than your competition? Do you want to pay 90 percent of medical coverage or only 50 percent? What about vision, day care, telecommuting, and flextime? Be forewarned: If you are not competitive, it will be harder to attract the key employees who are so much in demand. For example, some companies accrue sick leave, vacation, and personal time by the number of days worked. Some simply provide a number of flexible days off at the discretion of the managers, to be used for any reason whatsoever. It is important to

Benefits at a Glance

Medical Insurance

- The company offers family or single medical coverage with Blue Cross BlueShield under the Blue Choice New England plan.
- 100% of the premiums are paid by the company

  Blue Choice New England is a point-of-service (POS) plan, which means you pay less when your care is provided or coordinated by your network primary care physician (PCP).

Dental Insurance

- The company offers family or single dental coverage with DeltaPremier.
- 100% of the premiums are paid by the company.

  DeltaPremier covers 100% of most preventative (or Type I) procedures and 80% of basic restorative (or Type II) procedures up to a maximum of $750 per person per calendar year.

401(k) Retirement Program

- All employees are immediately eligible for the company's 401(k) program.
- The plan offers a wide range of investments from 14 different mutual fund families.
- Enrollment, account status, transfers, and changes are controlled by the employee.

Long-Term Disability

- The company offers long-term disability through UNUM.
- The benefit is 60% of monthly earnings to a maximum of $8,000 per month.

Vacation/Sick Leave/Personal Time Off

The company allots 15 days per year for a combination of vacation, sick leave, and personal time off. Employees may take their time off at any time, with manager approval.

Holidays

The following are our nine paid holidays: New Year's Day, Patriot's Day, Memorial Day, 4th of July and day after, Labor Day, Thanksgiving and day after, and Christmas Day. Additionally, two floating holidays are granted at the beginning of each calendar year.

Figure 1-1: A "benefits at a glance" summary

remember that if an employee perceives she is fairly compensated and has a good benefits package to protect her and enhance her quality of life, it will be much more difficult for a competitor to pull her out of your company. Keep in mind that one's perception becomes one's reality.

After your company reaches a certain size, you will probably need a full-time benefits administrator. In larger companies, you might employ an entire team of benefits people as a part of your human resources department. In start-up or smaller companies, it is a good idea to outsource your benefits management to a consultant who specializes in this area. This consultant will evaluate a company by looking at the number of people in the organization, assessing the current benefits plan and its cost to your company, finding out what your growth plans might be, and come back with recommendations. Very often this service is free because the benefits consultant is compensated by the organizations that he or she deals with when changing benefits providers.

Three final thoughts on benefits:

▸ Usually the very best companies have the very best benefits. They also have some, but not all, of the very best employees. This is no coincidence.

▸ Employees appreciate a good and comprehensive benefits package. I have seen employees go to other companies because of the benefits package being offered. They may not leave as often as they do for compensation issues, but benefits clearly play a significant role in decisions.

▸ The type of benefits package your company provides for its employees clearly sends a message about how the organization feels about its employees. In the highly competitive world of IT/Technology hiring, the message should be a good one.

It is extremely important to understand that benefits are a strong tool that attracts employees, and benefits should never, ever get in the way of making a hire. If there is a preexisting medical condition that might cause problems for the new employee, then you and your benefits people must figure out a way around the problem. If a candidate has three months left in her pregnancy, but the new medical plan will not accommodate the "preexisting condition" then you can pay for the candidate's COBRA coverage until the preexisting condition no longer exists. If a candidate has four weeks of vacation in his current job, but the position you are offering allows for only three weeks, it is important to see that the one week of vacation is not a deal breaker. Have the manager and the employee quietly work out an arrangement that will work for all parties. You could have been spending months to search for this candidate. Allowing one week of vacation to kill the deal is not a prudent business decision. Just be aware that if an exception to the general rule is made, never state it in an offer letter. It can become a precedent-setting action.

Position Profiles

I hate to be difficult, but position profiles must be completed for every open position that the company is looking to fill. Some companies even have position profiles already on file for every job in the company. This makes me smile, as I know their hearts are in the right place. But, naturally, profiles tend to age as business conditions and roles and responsibilities change. Many companies, of course, have nothing. Not a scrap of paper with any written information concerning the open positions. Here are some reasons you absolutely need position profiles:

Hiring is not easy Hiring is hard enough as it is. A position profile gives you a place to start that clearly illustrates exactly what kind of person you are looking for. Anything short of a good profile results in recruiters stabbing in the dark and having to guess about what it is you want.

Managers can be unclear about their needs Sometimes even hiring manages are not sure of what they want. So putting it into words on a sheet of paper forces one to think carefully and really pinpoint what skills one is looking for and what responsibilities are required of the job.

You need something in writing to show to the world When you are ready to begin the search, it is almost impossible to proceed without having a clear and detailed position profile to refer to. You need to let the world know what you are looking for. Agencies will not take you or your search seriously if you do not have a good position profile.

Candidates like to review the profile And this is a good thing. Candidates today are more sophisticated and very often ask to see the position profile. It reflects badly on the company if you have nothing in writing because it implies your organization lacks attention to detail and suggests you are not serious about filling the position.

Most hiring managers want help when it comes to recruiting and hiring, and developing a good position profile is the first step. It is difficult to get started because facing a blank page and creating a meaningful, useful document is a daunting task. And, of course, people are busy or traveling on business so much that they really have not had the time to think out in detail what they need. Recognizing this, Phil Sanborn of Management Solutions, a broad-based human resources consulting firm developed the Position Profile Template (shown in Figure 1-2). I have taken the liberty, with their permission, of customizing it for my clients, with great success. The beauty of this form is that it is nothing more than a collection of boxes that the manager has to fill out. When the boxes are completed, you have a position profile.

Position summary This is an area of the profile where the manager provides general information regarding what the new position is about and what the candidate will be doing.

Position responsibilities This is where the manager clearly outlines the day-to-day tasks the candidate will be performing and the types of activities the candidate will be responsible for executing. Do not exceed describing four or five responsibilities, if possible. Four is really the number to shoot for in terms of manageability. Yes, I know that we all do more than our position profiles would lead one to believe, but a long list here removes the focus from the most important areas of responsibility.

Specific experience Specific experience refers to the exact knowledge and background the candidate must have in order to be considered for the position. Specific experience usually, but not always, aligns itself with the candidate's responsibilities because he or she will probably not be able to perform the responsibilities without this experience. I recommend once again that you list no more than five areas of responsibility so that you keep focused on the most important factors. An endless list of required experiences just looks like a wish list.

Education This one is easy enough. Many positions will say BS/BA with five years of experience or equivalent. Try to be reasonable here. Education is important, but so are some of the intangibles like

Position Profile

Position title: _____

Reports to: _____

Organization: _____

Location: _____

Position summary (Write a brief overview of this position):

Position responsibilities (List between three (3) and five (5) specific responsibilities):
1.
2.
3.
4.
5.

Specific experience (List skills, knowledge required, specific applications):
1.
2.
3.
4.
5.

Education:

Personal characteristics:(List personal attributes, e.g., good communicator, team player, etc.):

Figure 1-2: Position Profile Template

EQ (the softer side/people-skill-oriented counter of IQ), native intelligence, chemistry, and attitude. Consider these as well. Figuring out what makes a person smart is something of a hobby of mine, and I have seen brilliantly educated people from great schools fail. I have also seen it the other way around. Do not look at educational credentials only—keep in mind that you are hiring the entire person. Hire for attitude, train for skill. Please consider this motto strongly.

Personal characteristics You may think this is not important, but it is. This section allows you to add a personal touch to the position profile and lets you include some of the softer skills that are required to be successful in the position: the ability to mentor a group, leadership characteristics, communication skills, strong consultative skills, etc.

I am sure you can see the simplicity of putting the profile template to use. The challenge is convincing some hiring managers to see the value of its development and how it will improve the hiring process. If the job of convincing is your responsibility, using a blunt instrument is not the most prudent way to get your point across and may have an impact on your effectiveness with the organization. Remember, you want the hiring manager to see the value of position profiles. A properly filled out profile helps support the recruiting and hiring process by the very nature of its existence—it can be available on a desktop ready to be sent out to anyone who wants to look at all the requirements. This is much better than having to describe everything repeatedly to everyone who asks. You want to be consistent in your explanations and descriptions.

Here are three ways to get the template completed:

▶ Email the template to the hiring manager after a face-to-face meeting, reviewing it first in hard copy and demonstrating how easy it is to fill out.

▶ Sit with the manager and have him or her fill out the template as you both discuss the position. This tends to work for managers who really do want to complete the profile, but tend to put everything else first before actually doing it.

▶ This one is a sure-fire solution. Take the manager to lunch to discuss the position, whip out a pen, and fill in the blanks as the manager talks. This works well because the free-flowing conversation allows the manager to discuss the position while you actually do the work of filling out the profile. Everyone ultimately wins here.

Regardless of which tactic you use, it is always best to review the position with the manager before you begin the task of searching and recruiting. Ask the following question: "Are you absolutely sure this is the type of person you are looking to hire for this position?"

Then put the profile in front of the manager for review or read it out loud. If the manager answers in the affirmative, you have succeeded and can move forward in your attempts to fill the position. If not, make the necessary changes, ask the question again, and move forward only when the manager agrees with what is down on paper.

If Recruiting Is *Your* Responsibility

Recruiting, like so many other functions in the corporate world, requires one key element: a driver. A person who is willing to stand up and say "I am the person who is going to make this happen!" Use the strategically designed and approved hiring plan, develop the hiring strategy and process, put all of the administrative infrastructure in place, and be the person who does the heavy lifting. The whole hiring process can be compared to fuel for a car. No matter what kind of car you have or how sophisticated that car might be, if you have no fuel, the car will go nowhere. Likewise, if you don't have an effective hiring process, your company will go nowhere.

This "driving" force happens to be necessary to every function that exists within your organization. Sales, marketing, operations, and finance are all members of the same driving club. Corporate America is filled with people who are unwilling or unable to drive the process necessary to fulfill the functions of their duties. Some pretty impressive people at very senior levels are not doing what is necessary to drive the processes that will result in the successes all of us expect. The point here is that if the hiring process is your bailiwick, it is imperative that you do not become one of the individuals just described. The process will not drive itself. If you assume the responsibility, drive the process and act as the fuel for this awesome responsibility. The results will be quite impressive.

Recruiting requires many things: judgment, people skills, native intelligence, stamina, the ability to resist choking certain individuals (diplomacy), patience, and at the appropriate times, impatience. Most of all, you must have the ability to keep the collective engines of the process running as you juggle a host of different balls and keep them from hitting the ground. This takes the capacity to come to work every day, prepared for the worst and hoping for the best. Be prepared to be the primary driver who makes things happen, be willing to manage and oversee the process, and be somewhat unreasonable in your expectations of others. It is okay to be somewhat unreasonable in your expectations of others. Recruiting is a service-oriented endeavor and is most often an unreasonable one. I know because I am involved in this work on a regular basis and have been told I can be something of a pain. I consider this a compliment because I achieve results, make friends, and form long-term client relationships. Work hard to build your company with the right workforce and watch your organization grow, prosper, and take flight. It is a grand and noble purpose that can be the beginning of a wonderful business-building experience.

2

Candidate Generation: Where to Find the People

First, you must find good candidates who you can turn into good employees. Sound obvious? Perhaps. But if recruiting is your responsibility, the glory comes with each new hire, and each new hire is predicated on an endless stream of candidates. We all know that in business, the more prospects, the more sales. The same principle applies to recruiting. The more candidates, the more people to interview and hire. Want to look like a hero to the company? Generate as many candidates as possible and then follow the established hiring process. Here's a saying to remember: Recruiting is the hardest job in the world if you work it easy, but the easiest job in the world if you work it hard.

On that note, here are the two main requirements of successful recruiting:

- ▶ A commitment to continually searching for new and creative ways of generating candidates

- ▶ A voracious appetite for generating as many candidates as possible

But, being successful is not as easy as it seems.

Why It's Difficult to Find Candidates

Finding good candidates is never easy. The amount of people who send in résumés and flood your inbox with email can seem endless. Recruiting can become quicksand as you try to locate the 9s and 10s among all of the résumés that come to your attention. Consider the following:

Candidates hide Many candidates do not wish to be found. They don't answer their phones at work. They check voicemail at noon and at the close of business, deleting all recruiting-related messages as soon as they receive them. This is not as unreasonable as it sounds once you understand that they get seven or eight calls a day. Some get more, including an architect who told me he had to get a second phone line installed because every other call was from a recruiter.

Employment options are plentiful Despite a temporary slowdown in the technology world (a market that I believe will come roaring back shortly), qualified IT professionals are still in great demand and tend to drive the marketplace. With the utilization of the Internet as a significant tool for job seekers, things move at warp speed. I get three or four emails per day, promising endless flows of candidates if I just buy this membership, post on that board, or purchase a new database to list all of my open positions on a zillion search engines. Naturally, each offer is special and for a limited time only.

The promises are overwhelming, everything from new technologies that will find candidates while you sleep to lists of contractors who are identified by skill sets. The business of finding candidates has taken on a bizarre carnival-like atmosphere that very often wastes far more time than it saves as the recruiter tries to figure out which services are worth looking at and which are not.

Stiff competition for good candidates There will always be the battle to beat the competition for candidates who meet specific requirements. This fact doesn't change despite how good (or bad) the economy may be. I have lived through a number of economic cycles, and I can assure you that good people are always hard to find. Common sense might dictate that people are easier to hire during lean times, but my experience in the trenches says otherwise. Oh sure, you might get lucky and get an easy hire or two, but that is the exception, not the rule. Recruiting becomes harder the more candidates you have, as your time is wasted by mounds of paperwork, special offers, nonstop faxes, and endless emails from candidates who aren't the right fit. I recently had lunch with an HR VP who told me he received 97 résumés over one weekend and gets almost 50 per day. Who has the capacity to rank, sort, and prioritize all those résumés and candidates? To guide the process, it is helpful to group candidates in three categories.

Types of Candidates

Candidates come in all different shapes and sizes but they are basically broken down into three different categories.

The Active Candidate

This job seeker is actively looking for a new position. She may be unemployed, unhappy with her current employer, or frustrated with the commute. She may be working on a project she hates, feels underutilized, undervalued, bored, in need of a change of scenery, wants more money, or it could be any of a million other reasons. The active candidate is the aggressor looking to find you and a listing of the positions that your company currently has available and wants to fill. Some people see the active job seeker as less desirable than the passive job seeker. Why? Well, how good can a candidate be if she is looking for another position and has her résumé out for the entire world to see?

Prejudging candidates before *truly* assessing them is, of course, patently ridiculous. *I* have been an active candidate! Some of the very best candidates I have ever met were also active candidates. Case in point: A client of mine was looking for mainframe candidates at a job fair eight years ago. (Job fairs, of course, are full of active job seekers.) I managed to drag "K.S." to the fair with me by luring him with promises of beer and fatty cocktail cheese puffs that were sure to be offered at the party following the event. Shortly, we met "A.N." I chatted with him and suggested he speak with K.S. Within a few minutes, K.S. was convinced that A.N. was the best UNIX guru he had ever had the pleasure of meeting. Then panic set in. There were 100 companies represented at the job fair, and surely someone else would also discover A.N.'s extraordinary skills. We managed to interview the candidate in a quiet area of the hall, had the candidate in our office the next day, did reference checks, and immediately made him an offer. He accepted, I looked like a hero, and K.S. is *still* happy as a clam and thankful that he had gone to the job fair with me. Make no mistake. Active job seekers run the gamut of being the very best and the very worst you can hire (just like passive job seekers). Anyone who says job fairs do not work is wrong. Job fairs don't pack them in just for the bean dip and Budweiser. Learn how to make use of job fairs in the right way (more on this later), and you will make hires.

The Passive Candidate

The passive job seeker usually posts his résumé in a database and is looking at your postings on the Web. He might respond and he might not. He or she is an elusive character driven by the winds of change and hopes for opportunity. These job seekers see this passive searching as a way to manage their careers. They fascinate us because they are something of an enigma. It used to be that you were either looking for a job or you weren't. Period. Passive job seekers create a whole new category of candidate that is *kind of* looking, but not *really* looking, all at the same time. They are almost always employed, relatively happy with their present jobs, and are looking just to see what is out there. Therefore, they can clearly be temped to change jobs if the right opportunity comes along. Generally, the "right opportunity" means "more money." Benefits, location, technology, perceived career path, and other perks also play a role, but for most people, the money is it. If you think this sounds cynical, think about the last time you met someone who made a lateral move or took less money for the "right opportunity."

Some passive job seekers practically make a career out of looking and interviewing, often during work hours. (This means they do it on your time, not theirs.) They spend a good deal of time on employment-related boards, looking up companies that interest them, entertain calls from headhunters, and are continually on the prowl. Passive job seekers tend to be of more interest to us because they tease us with the possibility that for the right opportunity, they will join us. They are harder to catch because they are not *really* looking for a new job, which seems to make them more desirable. They come in all shapes and sizes, ranging from the game player to the candidate who has a genuine interest. As usual, be very careful when evaluating candidates. Some are nothing more than extreme opportunists who will be surfing the Web within the second week of their new job at your company.

The Graymen

Graymen is a slang term for candidates who have been with the same company for more than nine years. The origin of the term is debatable, but my best sources tell me it was coined in the early 1970s by a giant computer manufacturer in Armonk, New York. Many graymen (or *lifers*) will not leave the comforts of their company. Job security, loyalty, fear of change, and a kind of ennui that sets in—all contribute to the feeling that makes one not want to leave his job. Because of the changes since the 1970s, there are very few graymen left, but they are still out there. When the giant companies began to lay off workers in the late 1980s, and "company loyalty" became a concept that was no longer viable, many graymen went to smaller, more rapidly moving companies in an attempt to survive. Some tried consulting or took early retirement. I mention the graymen because you should be aware of their existence. They may grouse, but often will not leave for love or money. Sometimes we get excited when we come across a grayman because we perceive he will have a great deal of experience and collective wisdom to pass on to us. In some cases this is definitely true, but be advised that sometimes twenty years of experience is nothing more than five years of experience…times four.

Your Mission, Should You Choose to Accept It

When attempting to generate potential hires, you must attract and evaluate both the active and the passive candidates. Between them are some of the very best candidates available to you, and it is your responsibility to identify, attract, and hire them to meet your corporate recruiting objectives. It is my job to teach you the methods I have used successfully, provide the pros and cons of each method, and help your to develop solid skills so you can effectively judge where to spend you valuable recruiting dollars. After you get comfortable with the different methodologies of sourcing candidates, a pattern of best practices will emerge for you. If you look before you leap when spending recruiting dollars, you will achieve a greater return on investment and begin to develop a history of what works and what does not. You will also gain credibility among the people within your organization when you begin to achieve results. Keep in mind, however, that the methodologies that provide you with great candidates at one time may not get you the same results at another time. Here's why:

- ▶ The shifting demographics of the changing workforce.

- ▶ The different types of candidates you are looking for within the IT community have unique requirements. (For example, would you necessarily use the same recruiting methodologies to look for mainframe programmers as you would for Internet developers?)

- ▶ Seasonal changes affect how people make use of time.

- ▶ The differences in the specific level of candidate you are trying to hire.

Being Aware of Options

There are all kinds of ways to find candidates. Some are tried and true, and some a bit flaky. To this day, if I dial a wrong number, I take advantage of the situation and inquire whether he or she knows of anyone who would be interested in/qualified for/looking for the type of position I am trying to fill. The person almost always talks to me. Just over the last few months, a similar strategy paid off for me. The sheer size of the facility where I now work makes finding company offices very difficult. If someone looks lost, I ask what company he or she is looking for. (I always seem to be able to tell within four seconds whether a person is on his way to an interview.) At this point, I take advantage of having a slightly nervous, somewhat confused technologist right there in front of me. I point the way to the company he is looking for (I don't tell him that the company has gone out of business. Really. I have stopped doing that.), then give him my card and tell him we are *also* looking for people to hire. I invite him to stop by later for some coffee so we can talk about how the interview went. The candidate almost always comes back to see me.

Is this method a good way to generate candidates? Well, perhaps not in the traditional sense, but you can either be the first person to try on a new style that may work, or play "follow the leader." Why fight for candidates using the same methods as your competition? It's your choice. You have to see the candidate as a customer, and in doing so, see the need to build trust and develop a relationship from the get-go.

The Importance of Tracking Candidates

Your first step toward crystallizing a successful candidate generation methodology is a solid knowledge of the current process your company is utilizing. How are you securing your new employees? Answering this question will help you analyze what is working well so far and what is not, and will also give you a picture of how you are spending your recruiting dollars. Before you pull the plug on any program, be sure to give each one enough time to get an accurate picture of its success or failure. Armed with that knowledge, you can develop a template (Figure 2-1) that keeps track of your new hires and what sourcing methodology you used to bring them into the company. In this way, you can see which sources are delivering and which ones are not. Figure 2-1 should be modified to fit your organization's needs and ways of doing business. Some of my clients skip the template and enter the information directly into a database. This also works as long as you make it a point to consistently perform this task. In my opinion, nearly all mainstream databases are sufficient, but Microsoft Access and FileMaker Pro are ones that I have seen utilized most often with good results. Designing your own proprietary database is also fine if it meets your needs and provides you with the data to make informed decisions. A personal request: Please do *not* use a spreadsheet for a database. When I see a client do this, I cringe. A spreadsheet is for numbers. A database is for storing data and slicing and dicing it in ways that will yield reports that will, in turn, provide you with pertinent information, enabling you to make insightful decisions. Databases, if used properly, turn data into information and information into knowledge. Spreadsheets are not equipped to perform the types of functions you will need with the level of sophistication you will require.

Once you are armed with the information you have gathered, it is important that you continually evaluate where you are spending your recruiting dollars. If a method is consistently not working after repeated attempts and tweaks to get it right, drop it and put more dollars into something that is working. It is extremely important to review your candidate generation information quarterly, at the very least. What might have worked last quarter might not work this quarter because of the endless employment and demographic variables that are in play.

Those in charge of recruiting must remain up to date in the latest candidate generation methodologies. There is often more hype than substance, and you need to learn to discern the difference. Stay on top

Candidate Generation Selection Worksheet

Category	Specific Source	Employee	Position
Job fair	Brass Ring		
Newspaper advertisement	*Washington Post*		
Job posting	Headhunter.net		
Database search	DICE		
Online career fair	Monsterboard		
Newsgroup	Programmers USA		
Agency	ABC group		
Search firm	Collins		
Employee referral	Tom Rogers		
Networking	Joe Allan		
Recruiting reference	Howard Adamsky		
Former employee	Tom Post		
Outplacement firm	Tompkins		

Figure 2-1: Candidate Generation Selection worksheet

of what is going on in your industry. Attend trade shows. Peruse newsgroups. Communicate with peers. Join local associations. Cruise the Internet and have an open mind. People who are selling a new methodology or tool will offer a great introductory price for the user to take a test drive. If a service sounds good, consider giving it a trial run.

Use Different Methodologies Concurrently

Do not use only one candidate generation methodology at a time. Methodologies work best when you have synergy—and give the various methods an opportunity to work together. One at a time, the results are slow. Running different methodologies simultaneously is the better way to produce good candidates. For example, when participating in a job fair, you could run a print ad to promote the job fair and also do some carefully planned radio spots to support both the job fair and the ad. You could even put up a banner on your website, announcing the existence of all three promotions, and run a contest for candidates who respond to the ad, show up for the job fair, or send in a résumé according to the radio spot. Doing all three is a far more powerful way to generate results *and* candidates.

As stated in Chapter 1, a company's success is dependent on having solid relationships with your business partners. No one succeeds alone. Because I practice what I preach, at a moment's notice, I can get professional advice and counsel in any area of business: finance, intellectual property, recruitment, advertising, accounting, benefits, web design, public relations, compensation, or anything else I might need. These relationships are there for me and I am always there for them. These carefully cultivated relationships are vital to my success.

The Key: A Solid Relationship with a Recruitment Ad Agency

This key partnership that your company must develop and nurture has to be made carefully, deliberately, and with sound judgment—the same as with all your other business partnerships. A reliable and effective full-service recruitment advertising agency is essential to the overall success of your candidate generation process. The purpose of recruitment advertising agencies is for far more than placing ads for you. They can also support you by

▶ Acting as a sounding board on recruiting ideas

▶ Researching employment websites

▶ Examining statistics on demographics for advertising purposes (radio, print, etc.)

▶ Seeking out and evaluating searchable candidate databases (i.e., places where candidates post their résumés) that are available through the various job sites found on the Internet

▶ Recommending the best times and places to advertise

▶ Administering your entire employee referral program, which will be described later in this chapter

▶ Keeping you informed of what methods the industry is using to unearth candidates

▸ Developing "slicks" (large, colorful boards used at recruiting events, which include your corporate logo and list all of your open positions)

▸ Developing any support material your company can use for recruiting purposes

▸ Being the people you blame if you don't make your recruiting numbers

My last remark, of course, is tongue in cheek. But the rest of the list is only a small sample of all the value that can come from this valuable resource. The advice, support, creativity, and services of a solid, well-selected recruitment advertising agency are absolutely essential to your company's recruiting success.

Choosing a Recruitment Advertising Agency

This is not difficult, but you must not be in a hurry. If you are, you will soon realize "There is never time to do it right but always time to do it twice." Choosing the wrong recruitment advertising agency will cost you time and money. You will have to start all over with a new agency that will have to reinvent your recruiting image and strategy, and then spend time familiarizing itself with your company and its culture. How do you determine whether an agency is not living up to your expectations? When it does not support your overall hiring objectives, need for service, and creativity, or when it does not fit your work culture or business philosophy. Remember that the work your agency performs is a creative process, and the agency is performing a service for you. Your agency is not a manufacturer that makes widgets. The relationship needs to be a close one that includes a deep level of trust and understanding. Your agency should be strategically tied to your organization's overall objectives. However, this relationship does not have to mean that both parties will agree on strategy and tactics all of the time. In general, you should know what you want. Your agency should know how to get it.

When Your Agency Is Not Working Out

Even if your recruitment advertising agency does not seem to be supporting your objectives, it pays to give the relationship a bit of time. In a meeting with the agency, identify the problems that exist and determine whether there are ways to resolve them. It is wise to remember that the fault almost always lies with both parties. The issues can involve communication difficulties, poor interpersonal relationships, or unrealistic expectations on both sides. It may take one meeting to hash out the problems (doubtful), or it might take five. Ultimately, your organization must designate someone to take responsibility to make the decision to pull the plug and find another agency, or to continue on with the current partner. Once a decision is made, it is best to make your move quickly. In the fast-paced world of IT, it is fatal to do otherwise.

If you decide to stick with your agency, do not consider pitches from others with the intent to motivate your agency to improve. This will only serve to create more bad feelings, complicate the relationship, and demoralize your current agency. It is okay to look at other recruitment advertising agencies even when relationships are solid, as long as you let your agency know you are doing so. Agencies do talk among themselves, and sooner or later, your agency will find out. When this happens, the trust you had built will be very tough to rebuild.

If the decision is to terminate the relationship with your agency, handle it in the same manner as you would with an employee. Do it quickly and fairly, with no finger pointing or accusations.

Choosing a New Agency

Here are some tips to help you when the time comes to hire a new agency:

- ▶ Don't hesitate to contact an agency that handles an advertisement or concept you like.

- ▶ Talk with people in your industry and find out whether they are happy with whom they are using. However, be careful about talking to your direct competition. They may not be overly willing to provide you with information regarding their recruitment advertising successes.

- ▶ Look at trade publications like *AdWeek,* which highlights key players in the ad industry. These key players are always looking to take on new clients.

- ▶ Do research to identify the key players in the recruitment advertising world. Contact them and let them know you are looking for a new agency.

Meeting with the Agency

This first meeting with an agency should simply be informational. It is important that the following people attend the meeting:

- ▶ The hiring managers who will be depending on the agency for advice and support.

- ▶ Senior human resources executives who will be interfacing with the agency on a regular basis.

- ▶ Marketing and public relations executives who will help the agency develop the reason why people should work for the company.

- ▶ A senior technologist who can translate techno babble into a meaningful dialogue with the agency's representatives to make them understand the technology that your company employs. (Remember, one of the purposes of the meeting is to get the agency excited about working with your company. The more excited they are about the chance of working with you, the better the job they will do in all aspects of their work.)

- ▶ The highest level of senior executive whose main purposes are to give a 15 to 20–minute pitch to the agency and answer questions.

- ▶ Anyone else who can add value to the meeting by providing the agency with information about your organization. The more information you provide to the agency, the better job they can do in developing a plan that makes sense, is cost effective, and achieves agreed-upon objectives.

Talk to More than One Agency

Describe some of the challenges your organization is facing and what you perceive the needs to be. The agency should outline its qualifications, history, client portfolio, and services it can provide for you. Do not automatically choose the first agency you meet with—making the right choice comes from looking at a host of different sources. I would not look at fewer than five agencies before making a final decision. When meeting with agencies, try to sample organizations of different sizes with different types of clients. Doing so will enable you to get a feel for who is out there, how they work, and what their capabilities are. Try not to be overly impressed by a long list of capabilities that you may not need. It is far more important that you take into account your recruiting plan, the budget, and your organization's hiring needs, and evaluate whether the agency in question can satisfy your requirements. Although this process may seem extremely time consuming, making the wrong choice will ultimately cost you much more time and money.

Selecting an Agency for "the Pitch"

I love that word. I love to hear agency people talk about how they are pitching and to whom. I think it's so exciting when the right agency matched with the right company sets an industry on fire, creates a memorable image, and reaches new heights of success that move an entire industry forward (e.g., the return of Steve Jobs to Apple, the development of the iMac, and the "Think Different" campaign). This example illustrates the importance of choosing the right agency, be it for advertising or recruiting. Before finally selecting a recruitment agency, invite three or four back for the pitch. (Do yourself a favor and try to schedule all of the pitches within one week, but not more than one per day.) The returning agencies should give presentations that include everything from sample print ads to a complete strategy that uses a host of different media related to your hiring objectives. The presentation could include pitches related to job fairs, radio spots, employee referral programs, and a full complement of strategic Internet recruiting concepts. It should be comprehensive and address all of your organization's strategic needs. Expect the pitches to vary based on the different experiences and types of successes each agency has had. Feel free to ask questions. If a recruitment agency has difficulty answering questions about their own plan, be wary. And, a last bit of advice—you will want your staff to meet the agencies' account executives because your primary relationship with an agency will be with them.

Bigger Is Not Always Better

Yes, big names tend to mean big muscle and extensive services. However, a big agency may not necessarily be the right one for you. If a smaller, local agency feels more comfortable and can meet your needs, then go for it! As your organization grows, your agency will tend to grow with you. Also, nothing against larger agencies, but they tend to have more turnover. What you want is a long-lasting relationship with your account executive. Trying to develop a trusting relationship with a new one every year is not the most productive way to get the results you want.

Sooner or Later You Have to Make the Choice

Making the final decision can be complex and based on a number of factors—some quantifiable, some not. Here are some points to keep in mind to help make your decision as pain-free as possible:

▸ Check references. Talk to the clients, the specific people who interact with the account executives you will be dealing with on a regular basis. Choose an assortment of clients, some old and some new.

▸ Check your comfort level—the chemistry is very important.

▸ Understand pricing. *You* are charged for the full price of an ad by your agency, but the agency gets a 15 percent discount from the people they advertise with. This arrangement is typical. Be sure you find out exactly what your agency will charge for all of the tasks they will be expected to perform. For example, if you ask your agency to research the best radio stations in Silicon Valley for drive-time advertising and report on the demographics with recommendations, find out what the price will be for that deliverable and how it is calculated. You don't want unpleasant surprises.

▸ Try to judge the agency by looking at what it will do for you rather than what it did for someone else. Track record is important, but you want the agency to support *your* goals. How will the agency get you from where you are to where you want to be? What is the proposed timeframe for accomplishing those goals? How much will it cost? Make sure the agency has provided you with the answers to these questions.

Final Tips

Do *not* do the following:

Demand exclusivity Demanding that the agency represent your company exclusively is unrealistic. Your agency wants the same thing you do: growth. Agencies aren't looking for product market share. They are recruitment advertising agencies competing for employees. It should be sufficient to have your agency sign a standard NDA (non-disclosure agreement), and it should have no problem doing so.

Ask embarrassing questions about other clients This puts your integrity on the line. Do not ask questions about how much other clients spend, how many hires they have gotten using different recruiting vehicles, and what their future plans might be. You can ask a question like "Do other clients have success using this type of recruiting?" but not "How many hires did Johnson Associates make off their Employee Referral Program in the first quarter of this year?" Doing so will put your agency in an uncomfortable position that could strain your working relationship.

Marketing's Relationship to Generating Candidates

Before we discuss specific candidate generation methodologies, you must understand marketing and its relationship to candidate generation.

I LOVE RADIO!

Here is an example that illustrates the importance of being known. I was recently asked by a client to advise on expanding an organization from 37 to 74 employees within 6 months. Translation: Double the size of the company in half a year. The organization had been doing brilliant, innovative work, but no one had ever heard of them. Recruiting was almost impossible. I suggested radio. The CEO happened to have a great voice and terrific presence, so I urged him to do the spots personally. (Doing effective voice ads is not easy to do.) After analyzing demographics to fit our audience, we chose two Boston-based radio stations and did three 60-second drive-time spots for a three-week period. Twice. The results were amazing! Keep in mind that we had the CEO speak straight from the heart about what his company does and why you should be a part of it. The personal touch and sincerity that came across made the listeners feel as though he was talking directly to them. In less than one month, we went from being a company that no one had ever heard of to a company that received countless calls and emails requesting information about available positions. The radio turned us into a player, which made all of our other candidate generation methodologies far more effective, because candidates knew who we were and what we did. Better yet, the message came directly from the voice of the CEO in an urgent call to action. Radio created such a buzz that it was the talk of the organization for over two months. I love radio.

The lesson:
Company awareness is as important to getting people in the door to interview as it is to getting potential clients to meet with your sales reps.

Marketing, defined in its broadest terms, is everything you do to promote your company or product. How you sell and to whom you sell fall under the marketing umbrella. The way your CMO positions your corporate image within the industry is marketing. Where you locate your business, the paint on the walls, the type of business card you give new employees, and the way they dress are all forms of marketing. In short, anything you do that the world will see or hear as it directly or indirectly relates to your organization is marketing. You may ask how marketing relates to recruiting. Well, there is indeed a relationship between selling your product or service to your clients (marketing) and selling your company to prospective employees (recruiting). Both are easier to accomplish if people have heard of you. And have heard good things about you. Simply stated, favorable public awareness of your company is extremely important and valuable. If your organization is an unknown player in your field, you will have a tough uphill recruiting battle ahead of you. If people do not know who you are, they will treat you with skepticism.

Now let's look at the different methodologies that help generate those candidates and see what some of the pros and cons are for each one.

Candidate Generation Methodologies that Work

Employee Referral Program

Employee referral programs (ERPs) are among the most powerful and effective tools your organization can use. In short, ERPs really rock! When I advise clients, one of the first things I ask is whether they have an ERP and how it works. Usually they pull out a policy manual, blow off the dust, and read something that sounds like this:

> Any person who recommends a candidate who is hired by our company will be paid a bonus of $1,000 after the new hire is employed for 90 days.

Woohoo! Now *that* sounds exciting, huh? Not exactly. Sounds B-O-R-I-N-G. This is not an example of the type of ERP I'm talking about. This was put together by some corporate representative who was simply following corporate guidelines. An ERP should not be a paragraph in a manual. An ERP should be exciting and inspire enthusiasm and participation. If you ask any employee within your organization to describe your ERP and he or she is vague or clueless, you don't have an ERP. You only *think* you have an ERP.

An ERP allows existing employees and new hires to recommend peers for employment within the company. Let me illustrate just how powerful this tool can be. In many start-ups, the first 15 to 20 people are very often hired as a result of an ERP. The great irony of this is that the company is so new there really isn't a formal ERP that exists on paper yet. However, the reason the "ERP" miraculously comes into being is that the enthusiasm regarding the start-up is so intense, people tell all of their friends, mentors, advisors, co-workers, and subordinates—anyone who is willing to listen. The excitement is so infectious that before you know it, the senior staff positions have been filled, as well as most of the remaining spots within the corporation. The people all know each other, the cost per hire is unbelievably low, and not an agency fee was paid. *This* is the power of an ERP.

How Do I Begin to Develop a Great and Powerful ERP?
Great ERPs are generally designed and executed most effectively by your recruitment advertising agency. Although I have seen impressive ERPs established by some larger companies, it is my opinion that you should leave the development of the ERP to those who make a living at it. Developing an effective, exciting, highly visible, in-your-face ERP should be a collaborative effort between you and your agency that keeps your budget in mind. Getting the program off the ground is the most expensive part of developing an ERP. After the initial work to get it up and running, the program needs only to be evaluated and updated every quarter, with perhaps a slightly larger tune-up after 18 months, according to your company's need for employees.

What Constitutes a Good ERP?
Let's cut to the chase. A good ERP meets the following criteria:

It is visible. *Visible* means everyone who works at the company knows it exists and can tell you what the payout is for referring someone who becomes an employee. It also means that it is not, as stated before, a policy in a corporate manual. It is a company-wide program that you promote with posters on the walls, includes special incentives like dinner for two if a candidate is interviewed, and awards a grand prize every month. Call it something different depending on the season. You are limited only by your imagination: Halloween Hysteria, May Money Madness, Sizzling Summer Bonus, The Great Winter Getaway to Somewhere Warmer than Here Contest, etc.

It is reasonable in its payout. *Reasonable* means it should be so in terms of how much the payout is *for the employee.* If your company wants to pay out $100.00 per Network Engineer, that is *not* reasonable. Numbers that vary between $2,500 and $4,500 per technical professional are not uncommon, and some companies pay even more for a second referral. If you think this is too much money, think again. An $80,000 candidate who comes through an agency that receives a fee of 25 percent will cost you $20,000. Do the math and you'll see that an ERP is a bargain.

It is communicated. The program must be communicated to the troops. Companies communicate in different ways—around the water cooler, in staff meetings, at gala events. Whatever the communication method, the ERP must be made known in an exciting way. Build up to the announcement of the program. Drop a hint or two a month before. If it is announced with excitement and enthusiasm, the results will be far better than if it is done by email and a posting on the cafeteria bulletin board. Make a big deal out of it and you will be pleased with the results.

Reward in Public

Remember the Management 101 rule? Criticize in private, praise in public. The same holds true for the ERP. If possible, meet once a month, talk about the hires, do a lunch, and give out the checks, awards, gift certificates, sporting event tickets, or car rental for a Ferrari for a week. Doing this in public is highly motivating for your staff. Remember, this program should be fun, visible, and exciting. As with most things in life, the more you put in, the more you get out.

Five Common Misconceptions About ERPs

First misconception People who work for your company should refer candidates for free. After all, if the company succeeds, everyone wins, so why should you give money for something like this? This thinking is brought to you courtesy of the "We Have Blinders on and our Heads in the Sand" club. It makes sense in theory, but in practice, no way will it work. As companies grow and become more corporate, the employee referrals begin to drop off. Money becomes the key motivator. Provide incentive and the people will follow. I can't tell you how many of my clients had no employee referrals until we instituted an ERP. Almost immediately, we received résumés, names, and email addresses. Another of my clients had an ERP called "Christmas Is on Us." It began in early November, and the bonus, paid to the referring employee, picked up the tab for the holidays. One employee went so far as to bring into my office, unannounced, not one, but two candidates. (We hired one.) Bottom line: Don't expect your people to do it for free when their peers at other companies are getting paid for it.

Second misconception If you give incentives to employees to bring in candidates, they will not do the work they are being paid for, and instead will spend all of their time looking for candidates. I have heard this argument only twice, both times from CEOs. I did not agree with them then, and still don't. I know of no company where this has been an issue. If you are running your company as it should be run, managing people effectively, and maintaining a healthy company culture, there should be no problems here.

Third misconception ERPs can't be changed midstream. Of course they can! This is part of the fun and excitement. Suppose your executive staff suddenly gets a large consulting assignment in Texas and you need 20 Internet developers pronto. What do you do? One of the first things you should do is communicate this urgent need to the troops and tell them there is an added incentive of "X" amount of dollars for each candidate. Make your people part of the solution. Tell them why the need is urgent and how their referrals will help. This is teamwork at its best.

Fourth misconception Managers are not eligible. Can someone tell me why not? Here we have some of the most experienced people in the company because of their connections, and they are excluded? This makes no sense. Include your managers. They deserve the same compensation and recognition as everyone else in your company. They also have the ability to help make your company the success it deserves to become.

Fifth misconception Awards should be given only if people are hired. This bad policy should be avoided. Employees should get small awards for trying. Yes, people should be paid for perform- ance, but active participation is the first step toward the per- formance you are looking for. For example, if an employee submits a résumé of a referral, the employee's name should go into a jar. At the end of the month, two or three names should be drawn for a prize. The more résumés an employee enters, the greater the chances of winning. Even small prizes like gift certifi- cates for dry cleaning, dinner for two, a golf shirt, or a Friday off mean a lot. If you are not sure what prizes your employees will like, poll your staff. They will be glad to tell you.

Take Your ERP to the World

Not long ago, I presented a great idea to a client: Let's pay $1,000 to anyone who brings us a candidate we end up hiring. My Aunt Millie, Prince Charles, Gunga Din, The Tooth Fairy, or anyone else. He didn't like it. "Why should I pay strangers for employees?" I answered, "Why should you *not* pay strangers for employees? Those checks you write out to agency people for $15,000 and $20,000. Are *they* family mem- bers?" His response: "Well, no, but that's their job." My reply: "Yes, that is their job. And our job is to see to it that we pay those agencies as few dollars as possible, do new and creative things to hire the employees we need, and not spend a fortune doing it." He was concerned about how we would look if we gave "money to strangers who did nothing except give us a name or a résumé." Even though I pointed out how we would be the envy of the free world if we paid only $20,000 for 20 employees instead of $15,000 for one, he was still unconvinced. Less than two weeks later, a giant manufacturer of computers set up a billboard on the Massachusetts Turnpike, announcing a $1,000 finders' fee for any- one providing an IT referral that the company hired. Can you believe it? Someone out there thinks like me.

A Sample ERP

Try this one on for size. It can be modified in any way that makes sense for your company:

- ► The Concept: Summertime Dreams.
- ► Timeframe: Memorial Day through Labor Day.

▶ How Communicated: Vibrant posters in high-traffic areas, paycheck stuffers, and an announcement at a company-wide meeting.

▶ Prizes: $3,500 per technical professional that is referred and hired, with that number going up by $500 for each additional hire in that timeframe. Dinner for two, even if your candidate is only interviewed. A weekly drawing for a day off, just for submitting a résumé to HR. A grand prize three-day get-away for two if your name is pulled out of the proverbial hat. Only those who referred actual hires are eligible for this one.

Pros

▶ Low-cost recruiting

▶ Generates excitement

▶ Beats paying agency fees

▶ Enhances corporate culture

Cons

▶ None that I can see!

The Internet

To begin with, here are some bits and bites about using the Internet as a recruiting tool:

▶ The Internet is here to stay. Learn to use it to your advantage and you will produce better results for your company, save money, and stay on top of the latest employment trends and technology for generating candidates.

▶ Understand how job sites have evolved. Not too long ago, they were not much more than boards to post open positions. Now they are full-blown portals with a host of services. Take a look at www.monster.com.

▶ Understand that a job site is, at a minimum, a destination site— where candidates and employers go to interact through job and résumé postings. As destination sites become more sophisticated, they might include searchable databases, career advice, résumé-building guidelines, online career fairs, and links to other sites to help employees, employers, contractors, and consultants connect.

▶ The hype on the Internet is endless. You will get bombarded by new and different deals that emerge daily. Learn to spot the trends that will get results and then discard the rest.

▶ Always include a link to your company's website. Even if it is an added cost, it will be well worth it to you and the job seeker. You will be more apt to interview a candidate who is well-informed and interested. Also, be sure the employment section on your website is easy to find, and all open positions are listed.

▶ Make sure that the person responsible for your Internet recruiting is trained by one of the leading Internet recruitment training services like AIRS (www.airsdirectory.com/news/). AIRS is an authority on the techniques, methods, and tools needed to successfully and creatively recruit candidates on the Web.

▶ Be creative and original when posting positions and responding to candidates. Do whatever it takes to interest the candidate in the open position. I find that the funny and the absurd work far better than the plain and ordinary.

▶ Do not limit your postings by listing only on the major recruitment sites. Also search for technology-specific sites and see if they will allow you to post positions. Some will and some will not. For example, if you are looking for a UNIX administrator, look for sites where UNIX administrators visit to post questions, chat, or do research. This is the perfect place to make your presence known.

▶ It is impossible to list all of the employment sites in existence. But I would be remiss if I didn't mention one of the best sites out there—www.myjobsearch.com. It is a compilation of the many job sites available, broken down by region and profession. It is a fantastic resource for employers looking for IT professionals. You can review the résumés of active candidates and post your open positions on a host of different boards at the same time.

▶ Remember that new employment sites are generated regularly. Use your favorite search engines to look for new and different employment sites. You will remain one step ahead of the competition in the never-ending battle to hire the candidates your company needs.

The Internet is a great way to attract both passive and active candidates. According to Jay M. Myer, formerly of headhunter.net and a leading authority on Internet recruiting, candidates spend a good deal of time cruising the Net to see what is out there. In a country where the technology unemployment rate can be as low as 3.6 percent in some regions, approximately 200,000 IT positions went unfilled in the year 2000. Knowing this, it should be obvious to you that quality IT professionals are still very much in demand. (Less than 4 percent unemployment is considered full employment by some standards.)

When people cruise the Internet looking for job opportunities, they notice what is out there, which in turn influences their opinions and behaviors. Because the Internet offers so much in terms of technology, speed, and opportunity for job seekers, I urge you to use it to your advantage to find the candidates. The Internet is an inexpensive medium to enter, and if you don't get results, it is an easy medium to exit. The Internet is also an instantaneous medium that moves at light speed. When a candidate responds to you, you must respond in kind, within less than a day. If you don't, you will be beaten out by all of the other companies that are on top of their game and have already contacted the candidate to set up an interview. If you are going to use the Internet for recruiting (as I strongly suggest you do), the first place to start is Electronic Recruiting Exchange (www.erexchange.com/). With more than 3,000 national and international members, it is a great place to get recruiting ideas, network, brainstorm, and make connections. It is a fantastic source for recruiters as well.

It is a challenge to keep up with the emerging and changing technology and tools that constantly birth new ideas and recruitment methods. Therefore, I will go over the methodologies that have worked well for me thus far.

Job Postings

When using the Internet to generate candidates, the first thing you should do is post your open positions. When you post on a destination website (a website where people go for a specific purpose, like job postings), candidates will look at the available positions and respond to your postings with their résumés. What a great deal. You are the one in control because the candidate comes to you; you don't have to seek out the candidates as you would have to in searchable databases (more on this later). Another plus to posting jobs on websites is that you will also attract the passive job seekers. Passive job seekers do not post their résumés in databases, so are difficult to locate. But if you are the one posting, and a job interests them, they will respond.

JOB POSTINGS WORK WHILE YOU SLEEP!

What a deal. You come into work in the morning and your inbox is filled with responses from candidates who are interested in your positions. And you didn't have to do any active recruiting! All you have to do now is review the résumés and determine which ones you are interested in. Posting job openings is much less labor intensive than searching a database. When you search a database and then stop to eat dinner, the act of searching stops. With a job posting, there really is no active work involved because the posting is up and attracting candidates 24 hours a day. You can be involved in other activities while the postings work for you. The need to respond quickly to candidates' résumés is, of course, critical because they are responding to the postings of other companies as well. Costs for job posting vary. Individual postings currently run about $300 with the premiere job boards, and more if you want to post on multiple locations or with multiple titles. Postings usually expire after 30 to 45 days. New boards sometimes give better deals to compete against the major players such as Monster (www.monster.com), Headhunter (www.headhunter.com), and Hotjobs (www.hotjobs.com). Some offer deals if you list more than a certain number of positions, and some will discount the price of using a searchable database if you spend enough money. Be advised that some sites will allow you to post for free, but they are usually less visible than the big sites. Less visibility means fewer candidate hits on the site.

Searchable Databases

Many active job seekers post their résumés on various website databases that specialize in employment. This is called a posting, but it differs from a company posting a position. This is a person posting their résumé for companies to search out and hopefully identify them as a candidate they want to contact for an interview. Some of the larger, more visible sites are once again, Monster, Headhunter, Dice (www.dice.com), and Hotjobs, but the list seems to grow daily. Searchable databases can be expensive, but that cost can be justified if it saves just one agency fee. If your company buys into one of these searchable databases, you will have access to countless résumés that have been posted by candidates who are actively seeking jobs.

Some databases have in excess of 800,000 résumés, and that number will only increase. If you happen to be looking for a software engineer and put in a query for C, C++, NT, and SQL, you might come up with 75,000 résumés to sort through and read. You can always change the query and narrow your focus. The search will result in fewer résumés, but the number will still be daunting. Who would read all of those résumés? (Not me.) Not only that, every other company that bought the database service has access to the same résumés you do, so the competition is tremendous. You will have to contact the candidate, get her interested in your company in 20 seconds, and assess her to see if she is a good fit. This is a tough way to do business. It is time-consuming and the candidate has all the control. Searchable databases do have some value. I have seen clients hire many good people off of these databases, and if your company has significant needs, this may be one way to go. My personal opinion, however, is that job postings are more effective. Pricing on database access can run as much as $10,000 or more for a year. Try before you buy. Many sites will give you a password for a few days to see what the database is like, or a 90-day trial subscription that will be credited to the full year if you extend the membership. Always try to bargain with the people selling the service because everything is negotiable. Beware of committing to a full-blown purchase. As an aside, a great site is www.free-for-recruiters.com. As the name states, it is free and allows you to browse the directory of résumés with hundreds of bookmark-ready categories.

Somewhat less popular but still of some value to recruiters are forums, newsgroups, and LISTSERV (defined in the next sections). They can help in finding candidates and making contacts, but you should always obey the rules that are made clear before you sign up for these services. Some allow job postings, some do not. If you observe the regulations, you will get along fine and will be a welcome participant.

Forums and Newsgroups

A forum or newsgroup is an online discussion group. Online services and bulletin board services (BBSs) provide a variety of forums and newsgroups in which participants with common interests can exchange open messages. Forums are sometimes called newsgroups or conferences.

LISTSERV

This is an automatic mailing list server developed by Eric Thomas for BITNET in 1986. When an email is addressed to a LISTSERV mailing list, it is automatically broadcast to everyone on the list. The result is similar to a newsgroup or forum, except that the messages are transmitted as email and are therefore available only to individuals on the list. LISTSERV is currently a commercial product marketed by L-Soft International, Inc. Although LISTSERV refers to a specific mailing list server, the term is sometimes used incorrectly to refer to any mailing list server. Another popular mailing list server is Majordomo, which is freeware (software whose license is awarded to the user at no cost).

Pros

▶ Low cost

▶ Covers lots of territory

▶ Used widely by job seekers

▶ Creates awareness of your company

Cons

▶ No guarantee of a hire

▶ Can be labor intensive

▶ Possibility of tremendous competition for each résumé

Advertising

To most people, advertising means the "Help Wanted" section of your local Sunday newspaper. This is, of course, a very shortsighted view of the world of advertising. There are many different places one can advertise, such as trade publications that cover your industry, newsletters from organizations that your employees subscribe to, and alumni bulletins that list positions to be filled. Where you choose to advertise should be based on the type of candidates you want to hire and where the specific interests of those candidates lie. People looking through the want ads are either actively looking for a job or seriously considering it (the active job seekers). This makes want ads the perfect place to find active job seekers. The negative? You will tend to receive more quantity than quality. In all likelihood there will be fewer than one in ten résumés you will want to consider. Finally, because of the sheer volume of advertisements, there is a tremendous degree of competition for candidates. Candidates may also miss seeing your advertisement if it is not eye-catching. If advertising is one of the methodologies you choose, consider some of the following to maximize your results.

Have Your Ad Done by Your Recruitment Advertising Agency

You shouldn't even think of doing the advertisements on your own. Wake up and smell the…ink. This is a job for professionals, not for someone who has a desktop publishing program and is looking to make a name for himself. If you are a company that is marketing-oriented and serious about recruiting, have your ads professionally done. Recruitment advertising is highly specialized and it should be left to the experts, like your recruitment advertising agency.

Spend Money

Spend as much as your budget allows. The size, in this case, matters. The bigger the ad, the better. Visibility is the name of the game, and candidates miss advertisements if they are too small.

Say It Again

Consider repeating an advertisement in the following week's Sunday edition. If people see your advertisement with some degree of consistency, they are more apt to respond. Given the choice, I would rather spend $20,000 on two medium-sized advertisements than $20,000 on one advertisement that is twice the size. Be aware of promotions. Very often if you run an ad two weeks in a row, the second week is half price. This discount isn't always automatic. You must ask to receive.

Advertising Tips

A few tips on advertising:

- ▶ Never run a Sunday ad when Monday is a holiday because people often travel or plan activities for the three-day weekend. They may never see the Sunday paper.

- ▶ The best times to advertise are right after the New Year until July 4th, and then again right after Labor Day until about the second Sunday in December. It is at these times the world is really working in an uninterrupted manner. The Christmas season and summer months find people in a lighter mood with their minds on other things besides looking through the help wanted section of the local paper. (Approximately 20 percent of the work force is on vacation during any week in the summer, and August tends to be a bit worse than July.)

▶ If you run a Sunday ad, pray for terrible weather. People tend to stay in and read the paper during stormy weather. You don't want your ad to run on the first great beach day of the season.

▶ Make it easy for candidates to respond. Give fax and email information. Do not give out a direct phone number unless you want to be deluged with calls.

▶ Put your company's URL in the advertisement.

▶ Make sure that each position is described briefly. Use bullets. Long job descriptions give the candidate too much to read.

Pros

▶ Lots of candidates respond

▶ Awareness is generated that helps to promote your company

▶ Good chance of multiple hires

Cons

▶ No guarantee of a hire for the dollars invested

▶ Lots of administrative work dealing with résumés

▶ Can be very expensive yet yield no hires

Networking

Networking is great for making contacts and is often overlooked as an effective way of recruiting. Networking is easy, requires no great skill, can be fun, and can take place anywhere, including airports, seminars, events that are specifically designed for networking, and even while waiting in line at the movies. (I once recruited a Java developer while in line to see *Hannibal*.) Networking is really nothing more than getting the nerve to talk with strangers and asking a question like "Who do you know who might qualify for a software engineering position with a great company in Boston?"

Be enthusiastic. That is really all there is to networking. It is nothing more than being friendly, talking with people, and asking a few questions. Don't be discouraged if you're not always successful. Some people are shyer than others and may not respond. Remember, a good tip is not to ask *if* they know anyone for a job, but *who*. Asking a "who" question forces the person to try to think of a name, rather than simply answering "yes" or "no." If the person remains silent for a while, be patient and give the person an opportunity to come up with a name for you.

Pros

▶ Meeting people is always a good thing

▶ Low cost

▶ Always the possibility of a hire or a referral

Cons

▶ No guarantee of a hire or a referral

▶ Some people do not perform well at networking events

▶ Networking events usually take your entire evening and some can be a bit of a bore

Outplacement Firms

Outplacement firms provide advice, support, and counsel to any employee who has been displaced by events such as downsizing (layoffs) or reorganization. There was a time that participating in an outplacement program was looked down upon, but this stigma, for the most part, is a thing of the past. If you think that outplacement firms are full of second-rate citizens, you're wrong. Up until the early 1980s, there was a preconceived notion in the minds of some people that individuals making use of outplacement firms are nothing more than corporate castoffs—people who lost their edge (or never had it) and were banished to this place of seminars, testing, coaching, and networking. A second-stringer at best. This is simply not true. Recognizing this, most recruitment agencies maintain very close ties with the better outplacement firms in major metropolitan areas, with hopes of recruiting outstanding candidates.

Pros

▶ Virtually no cost other than time and initiative

▶ Good chance of recruiting talented candidates who are highly motivated

Cons

▶ No guarantee of a hire

Professional Organizations and Networking Events

These are some of the best places to network and find talent. Because of this, you should always maintain a list of people you meet at workshops, seminars, conferences, and trade shows. This type of networking can be very valuable, and you never know when you might need the services of someone on your list. Just as the best time to develop relationships with doctors and lawyers is before you need them, the best time to network and build recruitment-related relationships is before your need for employees gets critical.

Pros

▶ Can build a great list of contacts even if you don't need them now

▶ Might learn something from a featured speaker

▶ Could find a potential customer or future business partner

▶ Virtually no cost

Cons

▶ Might not meet anyone interesting, have a dull time, and eat too many of those little greasy cheese balls

Job Fairs

Job fairs can be hit or miss, but I am a true believer in them because I know just how to work the system for maximum results. I have been to job fairs that have yielded few candidates and no hires, and have also been to job fairs that have produced some top-notch people and more than one hire. Do not judge job fairs based on the number of hires they have produced. Judge them on the number of offers you've made. If you make three offers and all are turned down, the problem is probably with your company, not the job fair. Job fairs are a forum for meeting candidates. From there it is up to you. I have found job fairs to be excellent sources of IT professionals and consultants. It is not uncommon for there to be 900 to 1,500 people at some of the smaller job fairs, and many more at the larger ones. Last year I attended a job fair that attracted more than 10,000 people. My advice is to try one or two per year and see how they work for you. Some tend to specialize in one market or another, with the narrower specialties drawing fewer people. Certain job fairs are more common in different parts of the country, but two of the most popular ones are BrassRing Inc. (www.brassring.com/) and Professional Exchange (www.professional-exchange.com/). Both of these organizations put on great career fairs, have excellent websites, and do job fairs in a host of different cities throughout the country.

Locations noted for technology very often sponsor their own job fairs and are advertised in the Sunday newspaper. For example, *The Boston Globe* runs events called "Jobapalooza," which focus on the high-tech industry and attract the big companies and great candidates. A company called HSP Global (High Skills Pool Global) sponsors job fairs all over the world, including China, India, Ireland, and other countries focusing on the IT industry.

You increase your likelihood of "job fair success" if you do the following:

Bring hiring managers This makes a big difference. Often if you present a stack of résumés to hiring managers back at your home turf, most will be rejected. However, if you are working the job fair as a traffic cop and can introduce candidates to hiring managers on the spot, you will do much better. This way, both parties have the chance to get to know each other and form a more substantial relationship, very often leading to interviews. (By the way, if you see a representative from another company spend a lot of time with a candidate, grab the candidate after he or she is through and introduce yourself.) The bottom line is there is a much greater chance of managers hiring people they meet and speak with at job fairs than there is trying to get the absent managers to invite candidates for interviews based solely on résumés that you dropped on their chair the morning after. I know this is true because hiring managers have told me they have hired people that they would never have even interviewed if they had based the decision solely on a résumé instead of having met the candidates first.

Lure them with food Everyone loves to eat, and if it's free, they love to even more. Most of the better job fairs try to keep you from getting hungry, so they have an endless supply of food in the hospitality suites, and usually have a cocktail reception on the first night for exhibitors. Both hiring managers and potential hires always welcome free food. (Truth be told, I myself have tracked down candidates I was interested in and snuck them into receptions so we could talk further.)

Be prepared I have seen "professionals" attend job fairs with little more than business cards and a cheap suit! You must, at a minimum, bring the following:

- Position profiles of all positions you are looking to fill.

- A large, colorful slick that sits on an easel (provided by the job fair people), aimed at getting people's attention. The slick should, at the very least, include your company logo and a list of open positions, if possible.

- Some company goodies such as tee or golf shirts, chocolates, company pens and highlighters, or anything else you think candidates might like.

- Material (brochures or pamphlets) about your company.

- A notebook computer for demonstrations if it is appropriate for your company's products or services.

- A contest, like a chance to win a Palm or gift certificates to Amazon.com. Include a fishbowl so candidates can throw in their business cards for the chance to win a drawing later.

- Your undivided attention. You are representing your company. Be respectful and polite, even if a candidate is not what you are looking for. You may not remember the candidate but the candidate will remember your company.

Pros

▶ Many candidates to choose from; gives hiring managers a feel for who is out there and what they cost

▶ Can get multiple hires if you work the system and are aggressive

▶ Often, onsite searchable databases that can be accessed through the hosting job fair's intranet

Cons

▶ Can be a bit pricey

▶ No guarantee of hires

▶ Lost time for hiring managers

▶ Food poisoning from the greasy cheese balls

One final word on job fairs: Most run for two days, beginning at 3:00 P.M. and ending at 7:00 P.M. Do not leave résumés of candidates overnight. First of all, you should have set up the interviews immediately. Second, certain unscrupulous individuals have been known to steal them.

Agencies and Search Firms

These are good places to find the candidates you are looking for. What's the difference between a search firm and an agency? Here are some of the similarities and differences:

Similarities

▶ Both charge a fee, agreed upon in advance, for finding and placing a candidate.

▶ Both charge a percentage of the employee's total guaranteed first-year compensation. For example, if the candidate is going to earn $100,000 in the first year of employment, and the fee is at 25 percent, the agency receives $25,000. However, if the candidate is going to earn $100,000 and a guaranteed bonus of $10,000, the total compensation would be $110,000 and the agency receives

$27,500. (Some charge a flat fee. See the "Tips" section later in the chapter.)

▶ Both will need to understand your company, the position you want to fill, your company culture, and the type of person you are looking for.

Differences

▶ Agencies tend to charge a bit less than search firms (e.g., 25 percent versus 33 percent). However, some agencies are now charging as much as 30 percent.

▶ Most search firms demand exclusivity. Exclusivity means that the agency gets a retainer and does not compete with any other agencies. Even if a candidate from the organization that they are doing the search for comes up with a candidate, the company is, by contract, expected to hand that candidate over to the search firm for review and consideration. They are also paid whether the candidate is placed or not, and usually want one-third of the fee on the day they start the search, one-third within 30 days, and one-third within 60 days. The fine print in the contract usually states that they are paid to "find and present candidates." If you do not hire whoever has been presented, it is not the agency's fault, and it will still earn the fee. (In many cases, an organization will hire even if it isn't crazy about a candidate because it leaves a very bad taste in the company's mouth to pay a big fee and end up with nothing.) Not all search firms have this arrangement. Because there is a degree of variation within the industry, take care in understanding the contract arrangements before signing.

▶ Agencies tend to be better at finding hard-core technologists. If you need a person who can deal with UNIX internals in his sleep, go with an agency.

▶ Search firms tend to be better at finding the more visible people within the industry. If you need a strong CFO or VP of engineering, go with a search firm.

▶ Agencies understand that they are in competition with other sourcing methodologies, including other agencies, and are paid only if they make a placement.

As just noted, there is a line separating agencies and search firms, but over the last few years, that line has become blurred. Typically, agencies present appropriate candidates to multiple organizations in order to secure as many interviews as possible. Search firms demand exclusivity, a retainer, expenses, and tend to visit client companies on a regular basis to form relationships, understand the corporate culture, and issue reports on each search. As the line between agencies and search firms has blurred, we have seen many agencies succeed in "moving up the ladder" by successfully recruiting and placing executives, requiring retainers, providing reports, and asking for exclusivity. Clearly, the differences between agencies and search firms are not as pronounced as they were ten years ago.

Tips

Agencies and search firms can be of great help to your organization if you manage the relationship effectively and use them only when needed. Below are a few ideas that will make working with agencies smoother, more productive, and ultimately add value to the process of bringing in these third parties to support your staffing efforts. Please be advised that in almost all cases, both agencies and search firms will not refund any portion of the fee if the candidate is laid off, is quickly transferred to a different position, or the company ceases operations.

- ▶ Both agencies and search firms are very expensive, so use them judiciously and look at other methodologies first.

- ▶ Before using a search firm that you are unfamiliar with, check references very carefully. Remember, you will be locked into a contract.

- ▶ It is not a good idea to use more than four or five different agencies at a time. The volume of résumés you will receive from so many agencies will complicate and confuse the process.

- ▶ Good agencies will not inundate you with paper—only with good and qualified candidates.

- ▶ Always read the terms and conditions of contracts very carefully for both agencies and search firms.

- ▶ Some agencies and search firms will work not for a percentage of the candidate's first year compensation as discussed above, but for a flat fee. As a result, the agent doesn't have an incentive to show you only expensive candidates because no matter whom you hire, the fee is the same. This arrangement is preferred by many organizations because they know the total cost of the hire right up front.

▶ Try to establish relationships with both agencies and search firms.

▶ Everything is negotiable, but negotiate up front. Never try to negotiate after the contract has been signed. It is extremely unprofessional and bad business.

▶ Try to negotiate the longest guarantee possible on a candidate. (The candidate guarantee is the amount of time that a candidate stays with your company before a refund of the fee paid is no longer possible if the candidate resigns.)

▶ Arrange to receive a cash refund if a candidate does not work out. This will allow you to go to other agencies and find the best candidate, which makes it better than a replacement guarantee. A replacement guarantee means that the agency will not give you any cash back but will replace the candidate at no additional charge. If the new candidate's total compensation package is higher than the original candidate's total compensation package, you will have to pay the difference. For example:

> If the fee for the first candidate is $12,500 and the replacement candidate's fee is $13,000, the difference is $500, which you will be expected to pay.

The downside to replacement guarantee is that you have to work with the agency that made the placement as opposed to having the opportunity to try another agency. In reality, you were only given a credit equal to the fee paid based on the contract.

▶ Do not be pressured into hiring. Both types of organizations want to finalize a deal quickly because it is more profitable for them to do so—time equals money. Let these third parties find you candidates. Do not let them sell you candidates.

Pros

▶ Virtual guarantee of a hire

▶ Organization will do all it can to see that the candidate is the right fit to avoid multiple searches

Cons

▶ Very expensive

▶ Can be slow and tedious process

▶ Agencies can push very hard and try to rush the process

Recruiting the References of Potential Hires

When checking the references of those you plan to hire, try to strike up an open and friendly conversation. This can be a good lead-in to finding out whether the person you are talking to would also be interested in working for your organization. This person might be a good fit for your company and very receptive to the idea. It never hurts to ask whether he or she might be open to hearing more about your company over lunch or on a separate call. Even if uninterested, give this person your contact information and call again in three months. You never know what the response might be at that time.

Pros

▶ No cost on this hire

▶ Possibility of a great candidate

▶ Nothing to lose

Cons

▶ Person might be irritated or offended

Contacting Former Employees

It's a great idea to contact former employees who left your firm on good terms. They know you; you know them. Maybe there is a great project they would love to work on. Perhaps the extensive travel schedule you had them on has diminished. Give them a call and see how the new job is going. Take them to lunch and tell them how much you miss them. Be bold. Give them reasons to consider rejoining the company. Make a compelling argument about why they would be better off back with you than at their present job. Former employees who leave on good terms and return to a company tend to do well. They know the culture, the process, and feel right at home. Sometimes contacting former employees is looked down upon and can be hard to sell as a viable sourcing tool. As one manager said to me, "No way. If they left, why would they want to come back"? This attitude doesn't pay. There can be many reasons former employees would want to come back. It is up to you to convince them.

Pros

▶ Never hurts to ask

▶ No cost to hire

▶ Employee is a known entity

▶ Candidate loyalty is solidified

▶ Good for other employees to see

Cons

▶ None

College Recruiting

College (campus) recruiting is absolutely critical to an organization that thinks long-term and wants to *build* a great organization. Show me any company that is looking to stay competitive, and I will show you a company with a great (aggressive, proactive, highly visible) college recruiting program. It only makes sense. If the college students of today are the employees of tomorrow, you must identify the best and work them into your company. College recruiting is clearly one of the best investments you can make in your company's future. Consider this, too: Everyone would like to get the best students from MIT, Harvard, or any of the Ivies. But if you shoot only for students in these top schools, you will find the competition to be overwhelming. There are many state and lower-prestige schools that produce great candidates. (Look at me. I went to Brooklyn College and some people consider me relatively smart.) Throw one or two of the Ivies in if you like, but consider the Northeastern Universities and Worcester Polytechnic Institutes of the world. They turn out some truly great students that do wonderful work.

Pros

- ▶ Great way to ensure your future

- ▶ Get a shot at the best and the brightest

- ▶ Build awareness and public relations

- ▶ Brand your company

Cons

- ▶ Time-consuming

- ▶ Expensive

- ▶ Takes real planning, initiative, follow-through, and commitment

- ▶ No guarantee of hires

A Quick Word on Measuring Results

The results and success of a recruiting method are not measured by the number of hires. They are based on the number of offers. If many offers are made but not accepted, it is not the fault of the method. It is the fault of the company. Perhaps your compensation programs are not matching industry norms. Perhaps your benefits are not comprehensive enough. Maybe you are not good at closing the deal. There are many factors that can contribute to offers being turned down. The sooner you identify and correct the problem, the sooner you will meet your hiring objectives.

There is no way I can address all sourcing methodologies and the implications of each one. However, if you use this chapter as a guide, and enhance your tools for gathering new candidates and exploring emerging techniques, you will be able to compete successfully with all companies under all circumstances and achieve the results you want. Just remember that creativity, speed, and follow-up are all critical to making any candidate generation methodology successful.

3

Basic Interviewing Essentials

Interviewing is both an art and a science. It is a complex and highly sophisticated, involved interaction. Over my long career, I have heard many opinions about how interviews should be conducted: "They should be intellectually stimulating," or "It is best to make interviews amusing," and even "I only interview candidates while on my three-mile run at lunch." In one of my first consulting assignments, a hiring manager I worked with told me that people think at their best when high on endorphins. If a candidate did not run with him, he did not interview him or her. Although an "interesting" approach, not at all practical. He finally confessed to me that interviewing strangers in small rooms made him feel claustrophobic. Our solution was for me to coach him prior to an interview. I spent time with him and described interviewing as a task with a desired end as opposed to a casual conversation you'd have while running with someone. I also pointed out the importance of taking notes, which can't be done while running. This alone was probably the major change that relaxed him enough to conduct the interview. Furthermore, I suggested that he conduct the interview in a well-lit, large conference room rather than in his small, cramped office. After the interview, we met to debrief, which gave him the opportunity to talk about the interview, ask questions, and review the assessment sheet. These combined strategies helped him gain confidence for future interviews and was certainly much better for the interviewee.

Why Interview?

One can define *interviewing* in a host of different ways. But the following definition highlights why it is so necessary to participate in the interviewing process:

> Interviewing is the act of assessing the skills, experience, background, accomplishments, and knowledge a candidate possesses as it relates to the specific position for which that candidate is interviewing.

Even more to the point, the purpose of interviewing is to help the

- ▸ Company evaluate the abilities, experience, qualities, and overall appropriateness of the candidate, and what added value he or she will bring to the organization

- ▸ Candidate evaluate the open position, and the company's culture, history, current place within the marketplace, future plans, the position being interviewed for, or anything else that could help the candidate make an informed decision

Who Is Really Interviewing Whom?

An interesting question, and a good one. Both parties are interviewing each other. There was a time, of course, when this was not the case, and the company was the only one doing the interviewing. Those days, thankfully, are gone. To be successful in hiring the right candidate for your organization, there has to be a balance of power between the candidate and the person representing the company during the interview process. A one-sided relationship is not a fruitful one, and seldom results in a win-win situation. With necessity being the mother of invention, the IT community realized the importance of a more equitable interviewing process. It is in the best interest of each party to carefully and equitably evaluate each other so that the employment process works as it should. If the candidate is uncomfortable with any significant, irresolvable issue concerning the company, he or she should not accept the position. Naturally, if the company has similar issues with the candidate, it is best not to make that hire. This does not mean that everything must be perfect between candidate and company. It simply means that both parties must be comfortable enough with each other before moving beyond the interviewing phase. Take the opportunity that interviewing provides to air concerns, voice opinions, and pose the necessary questions. Doing so cooperatively will result in successful new hires, new opportunities, and the promise of great things to come.

The Successful Interview

Interviewing requires a bit of philosophy and the ability to follow rules that should never ever be broken. To help you become the comfortable, capable, successful interviewer, I have put together a collection of ideas, tips, and techniques that will enable you to determine who you should and should not hire. Armed with this information and a new outlook on the interviewing process, you will become better able to guide your organization toward the road to success. Even if interviewing is not your strong suit, the tips in this chapter should help make you capable at representing your company during the interview process. And your proficiency will increase with more interviews you do on a regular basis. Developing these strong skills is essential if you are going to provide your organization with an unbiased opinion you can justify. You must be able to complete the interview process accurately and fairly, which will enable you to assess the candidate fairly and accurately, and pass on the information to the interview team. By doing so, you will help your organization guard the employment door judiciously and let in only the best candidates.

Never Discriminate

This is Rule Number One for interviewing. Laws vary some from state to state, but the bottom line is discrimination is both harmful and illegal. If a candidate feels discriminated against and wants it to be known, he or she can accomplish that goal very easily by going to any number of organizations that will actively and aggressively investigate the allegations. Different states have different organizations, but the two that will be sure to get your company's attention are the Equal Employment Opportunity Commission (EEOC), on the federal level, and your state's Department or Division of Labor and Employment. These agencies have teeth and will use them. Discrimination against any employee based on race, religion, disability, age, sexual orientation, gender, or nationality is patently illegal. You can get yourself into trouble simply because of the types of questions you ask a candidate. For instance, if you interview someone who is blind, you may not ask if the disability will interfere with the requirements of the job, even if being sighted seems necessary to perform the duties of the position (e.g., a developer). Similarly, if a candidate is pregnant and will therefore not be available at a critical time in a project's schedule, you may not use it as a reason not to hire. However, you may ask what tools or accommodations he or she requires to do the job, or what level of success has been achieved in previous similar jobs. These situations are *very* delicate and laws do change. If in doubt, consult with a competent employment lawyer *before* you get into trouble as opposed to after.

The bottom line is that, even if practiced subtly or tolerated within your organization, discrimination will become a part of the company culture and an unspoken (though not unseen) way of doing business. Your employees watch you far more closely than you think. You can smile and talk about diversity in company meetings, but do nothing to achieve this goal and your employees will see exactly what is going on. Unethical business practices and lack of integrity will damage your company. Lead by example by learning the value of diversity and practicing it in your recruiting. Diversity in the workplace is a powerful tool that brings forth innovative ideas and enriches the workplace experience.

Worth Noting

Ask only questions relating to the position profile. Doing otherwise, depending on the questions you ask, may be against the law, unethical, and lead to lawsuits.

As the interviewer, it is your responsibility, and obligation, to make your hiring recommendations based solely on the criteria of the position. Everyone has an opinion about what kind of person may or may not do well in a position. Maybe you think the candidate is too old for the stresses of the job. Or a woman would be better in a customer services role. The reasons people give for the hiring decisions they make are endless. Instead, remind yourself that you are only to assess the skills, experience, background, accomplishments, and knowledge a candidate possesses as it relates to the specific position for which that candidate is interviewing. This is the way toward greater success within your organization.

Always the Two-Part Interview

When you interview IT candidates, you should always ask two types of questions: the non-technical and the technical. Let's examine both types of questions.

Non-Technical Questions

Non-technical questions uncover the candidate's work style, employment interests, motivations, work habits, personality type, and overall employment background, *not* the candidate's abilities or experience as it relates to the technical requirements of the job. For example, you might inquire about the reasons the candidate wishes to change jobs, what type of company he or she would ideally like to work for, or what he or she looks for in a manager. Those are important questions that need to be asked. Later in this chapter, I will provide a more comprehensive list of sample non-technical questions and why it is important to ask them.

Technical Questions

These questions pertain only to the technical aspects of the job. For example, if the candidates are interviewing for a developer position, it is perfectly okay to ask what languages they program in, how many lines of code they can write in a day, and what their favorite programming language is. These questions are important because they help the interviewer to assess the candidates' technical knowledge and capabilities.

The All-Important Phone Screen

If, after evaluating a candidate's résumé you are still unsure about whether to conduct a personal face-to-face interview, it is best to do a phone screen. A phone screen is really nothing more than a mini interview that can be done in 15 or 20 minutes. The call should help you to decide whether you will bring the candidate in for an interview. It allows you the opportunity to question parts of the résumé you may find vague, confusing, or incomplete. Has the candidate held many positions in a short span of time? Are there periods of time that are unaccounted for? Missing titles? These issues can be cleared up clearly and easily over the phone. As a matter of fact, phone screens are also recommended for candidates you think you are sure of. You might very well find that after a brief phone conversation, the candidate is not really someone you want after all. Phone screens are also very cost effective and time efficient, saving time for you, your staff, and the candidate. There is nothing more senseless and psychologically draining than doing all that is necessary to schedule and coordinate the interviews of four or five people when a phone screen could have determined that three of the candidates aren't qualified. Remember to always send an SAI letter as soon as you have determined that a candidate is not right for the job.

Worth Noting

To avoid the ramifications of disgruntled candidates, phone screen whenever possible rather than spending a hurried ten minutes in a face-to-face interview and then shoving the candidate out the door. This is bad business, and reflects poorly on your company.

First of all, there should be only one phone screen per candidate, and it should be done in the evening, usually between 8:00 and 9:30 P.M., including Sundays. If the issues needing clarification are of a technical nature, the hiring manager should conduct the phone screening. Otherwise, the recruiter should phone screen. As stated previously, the call does not have to take more than 15 or 20 minutes, although it can run longer if you wish. You should use the time to make absolutely sure there are no major miscommunications about the position and its responsibilities, the company, or the skill sets and experience of the candidate. The phone call is a great way to help you confirm whether the résumé accurately represents the candidate. Be sure to be friendly and upbeat during the call. In the end, the interviewer should feel comfortable making a decision about whether to bring the candidate in for an interview or not, and the decision should be final. If the candidate is to be brought in for an interview, contact him or her no later than the day after the phone interview. If the candidate has been ruled out, an SAI should be sent out immediately. In the long run, you will never be sorry that you did a phone screen. Lastly, avoid hiring a candidate with whom you have interviewed only by phone. This should be obvious to you, but I find it necessary to mention it here because some of my own clients have done this in the past.

Never Hire After Only One Interview

No exceptions here. Not for an old friend. Not for a relative. No one. One interview is never enough. Proper interviewing, evaluation, and careful analysis take time and are necessary to make a prudent decision. If you make a quick decision, you are giving up the valuable time you need to make the proper choice. Conducting more than one interview of a candidate is the best way to avoid hiring someone that you later wish you hadn't. Hiring managers have told me there are three primary reasons they hire on the spot:

▸ The candidate was immediately seen as being "perfect for the job."

▸ The hiring manager "fell in love" with the candidate.

► Desperation on the part of the hiring manager. This is addressed later in the chapter, but in short form, never hire out of desperation. It is short-term thinking and no way to build a long-term business.

This type of thinking is dangerous. Instead, if you feel this strongly about a candidate, confirm your impressions in a second interview, at a different time, with other interviewers. After I interview a candidate I feel strongly about, I let the other interviewing team members know how I feel. They know immediately that I am seeking their advice because I recognize I am blinded by my biases toward the person. I need others to tell me what it is that I am not seeing. There are no perfect candidates.

One final point: There are some people who think it is okay to hire non-exempt employees after only one interview. They see non-exempts as low risk, and are willing to give them a try because if they do not work out, they can be easily fired. This is no way to conduct business. It demonstrates short-term thinking at its worst. Instead of "trying out" people to see if they can cut it, hire correctly the first time and avoid all of the misery that accompanies firing people. It is terrible for morale, a waste of corporate resources, and extraordinarily insensitive. From a practical standpoint, you do not want to be dragged into court by an employee who feels he or she has been terminated unfairly. Do this with several employees and you will have a class action lawsuit on your hands. Even if the court decides in your favor, you still lose by paying thousands in legal fees, developing a bad reputation, and affecting the productivity and morale of your employees who will be discouraged by their organization's behavior.

Beware of Candidates Who Speak Ill of Their Former Employers

Interviewer: "Why did you leave your previous position?" Candidate: "Because those people were the biggest morons I ever met." Not a good answer, at least from the interviewer's standpoint. Even if the information is true, what an inappropriate thing to say to an interviewer! There should be, as my mother says, a big difference between what you think and what you say. Beware of people who badmouth their former company, bosses, co-workers, etc. You want people in your organization who have the sense and ability to screen and filter out patterns of behavior that are inappropriate for the workplace. You want someone who can work well independently and as a team member. Someone who cannot or chooses not to behave appropriately during an interview may be unable to form cohesive working relationships or handle conflict and differences of opinion well. They are more likely to be difficult to manage, highly mercurial, and tend to be what managers call "high-maintenance" employees who are at the root of many employee-relations issues. You may theorize that hiring a free-thinking "maverick" who seems bright and brutally honest may be good for your organization. Do not give in to this temptation. These are favorable characteristics under the right circumstances and conditions, but do not use your workplace as the experimental lab to try out your theory.

Read the Résumé Twice Prior to the Interview

Do not read a candidate's résumé a measly two minutes before the interview. It shortchanges you, the candidate, and the company you represent. Here is a good test to see if you are familiar enough with a résumé. Do you have any questions for the candidate based on your review of the résumé? If you don't, you did not read it with as much attention to detail as you should have. Read each résumé twice. Remember, you are the keeper of the gate and must be selective about who you choose for your organization.

Ask How

Here is one good piece of advice that my friend Bill Shaw gave me. Ask the candidate how. And ask it over and over. "Your résumé says you increased sales by 67 percent in three days. How?" "How did you streamline marketing and make it 14 percent more effective while cutting overhead by 77 percent?" "How did you cut manufacturing costs by 7 percent?" How, how, how? The "how" question is key to confirming any information in a résumé claiming responsibility for an accomplishment. Did the candidate *really* set up a complete LAN by himself in just one weekend? Perhaps he worked with a team or simply made one phone call to a group of consultants to get the job done. As we all know, some candidates will exaggerate to beef up a résumé.

My last thought on this subject: "How" does not necessarily mean that the candidate must tell you the minute details of how he accomplished a task. It simply means that you, the interviewer, must be sufficiently satisfied that the person claiming responsibility actually was responsible for the listed accomplishments. For example, if I put on my résumé that I was responsible for writing this book, I would not necessarily be able to tell you in the minutest detail exactly how I did each and every task. However, I could provide a general outline of the steps I took to write this book.

Worth Noting

The biggest, most important piece of advice in this chapter: Understand to the best of your ability the position you need to fill! The interviewer must have a clear and concise understanding of the open position. Never conduct an interview if you do not understand the requirements of the position. It will be impossible for you to assess a candidate if you have no knowledge of what you are assessing the candidate against.

Ask What

By the end of the interview, you must understand what the candidate's accomplishments and roles were in his or her previous positions. Don't be afraid to ask for clarification if you are unclear about anything the candidate has stated. It is your responsibility and obligation to get the information you need to make an accurate assessment of the candidate. Sometimes it is helpful to repeat or restate your questions differently if the answers are unclear or if the candidate seems nervous. Look for specific, concrete information regarding achievements and daily responsibilities. Have the candidate break down the particulars into manageable bits of information in order to get what you need. Asking "what" will help you determine whether the candidate is a doer, a planner, or a hanger-on. Will this person power the ship or be a barnacle?

Responsibilities vs. Accomplishments

Responsibilities and accomplishments are not the same thing. For example, if I have a bulleted item on my résumé saying that I increased sales by 17 percent in 3 months, this is an *accomplishment* because I can tell you *how* I did it (added 3 new sales people, set up a telemarketing department, changed the compensation plan, etc.). This is very different from saying I was *responsible* for sales. The very nature of a statement referring to responsibility makes it difficult to answer "how." When a person describes an accomplishment, you can easily get an answer as to how it was achieved. If a person describes a responsibility, you must dig to find the accomplishments achieved within the responsibility. Finally, remember that just because a person makes a statement like "responsible for U.S. sales," it does not mean he or she was any good at it. I have known countless people who were responsible for many things and were terrible at it. Responsibility does not necessarily equal success. Instead, be on the lookout for past accomplishments because they are the true indicators of what a person will do in the future.

Check for a Sense of Humor

You want an employee who takes the work, but not himself, seriously. In the IT world, the pressures and demands are intense, and you can fall three weeks behind by taking two sick days. If you have a sense of humor, you have the ability to step away from a problem and put it into perspective. A sense of humor alleviates stress and makes difficult situations more bearable. This is key to being able to make good business decisions.

Sell the Candidate on the Company

Selling the candidate on the company during the interview process is critical to an effective hiring strategy. You want the decision to hire to be your choice, not the choice of the candidate. Therefore, make sure the candidate leaves the interview

▶ Wanting the position and hoping for an offer

▶ Excited about your company

If you can achieve these goals, more candidates will accept your offers because they won't want to miss out on the opportunity to work for your company.

Selling the company during the interview is not difficult, but there is a prerequisite: You must be comfortable doing it. It must become second nature. All that is required are two things:

▶ A genuine enthusiasm about the organization. Communicate it during the interview. Enthusiasm is contagious, and you want your candidate to catch it from you.

▶ Getting across what you like about the company and working there. Casually talk about the perks, the people, and the atmosphere— pizza and brainstorming sessions on Fridays, great people to work with, friendly environment, free technical training, etc.

About ten years ago, I worked for a search firm. One day, our president asked me to interview a candidate whom he really wanted to hire. During the interview, the candidate suddenly swung around in his chair, looked me in the eye, and asked *me* why *I* worked for the company. We stared at each other for a long time. I soon realized there was very little I could say that was positive, and couldn't sell the candidate on the company. The candidate and I both came to the same conclusion at that moment. There was no reason for me to stay with the company, and I opened my consulting practice. There was no reason for the candidate to accept the position, and he went elsewhere for employment. It was an eye-opening, life-changing day.

The Candidate Assessment Sheet

It is poor practice to take notes on a candidate's résumé. If you make the hire, the résumé will end up in the official file of the employee. But most importantly, you need some way of easily recording your impressions and assessments of all the candidates in a consistent format so that your hiring decision is based on comparable information and is defendable. The Candidate Assessment Sheet (Figure 3-1) allows you to quantify exactly what you think about candidates and their skills rather than making vague, general statements about them. Fill out each sheet immediately following every interview. Waiting to do so after a series of interviews could result in confusion and inaccuracies. The Candidate Assessment Sheet forces you, the interviewer, to think carefully and enables you to make comparisons among all your candidates so you can make the best hiring decision for your organization.

Worth Noting

The Candidate Assessment Sheet should mirror the position profile (discussed in Chapter 1). For example, if the profile states you are looking for someone knowledgeable in Java, Perl, HTML, and ASP, the assessment sheet should reflect the same skills. The position profile and the Candidate Assessment Sheet should *both* be used as a tool to help you determine a candidate's appropriateness for the position you are hoping to fill.

| Candidate _____ |
| Interviewer _____ |
| Position _____ |
| Date _____ |

Specific Experience (Skills, knowledge required, background)		**Comments**
	Circle	
	1 2 3	
	1 2 3	
	1 2 3	
	1 2 3	
Personal Characteristics		**Comments**
	Circle	
	1 2 3	
	1 2 3	
	1 2 3	
	1 2 3	

1–Below expectations; 2–Meets expectations; 3–Exceeds expectations

| **Overall Comments** |
| |
| |
| |
| Decision to pursue: Yes___ No___ |

Figure 3-1: Candidate Assessment Sheet

Never Stop Interviewing

Just because you have found the ideal candidate does not mean you should stop interviewing. Even if you are about to make an offer, do not let go of your options. I have seen candidates back out at the last minute for every conceivable reason, leaving the hiring manager with absolutely nothing to fall back on. For example, my good friend Richard Higgins tells the story of a man who was just about to get into the moving van to move to another state for a new job. The deal to take the job had been signed long ago. Meanwhile, his wife was found crying in the backyard, feeding the deer she had fed every morning for the previous five years. You can guess what happened to the deal. This type of situation can be very devastating for an organization, and emotionally draining, especially when trying to fill critical positions. Often, companies have spent months and a small fortune trying to find the right candidate. Keep the interview process going. Only when you make an actual offer (a commitment to the candidate), should you put all interviewing activity on temporary hold. During this "hold" on interviewing (the time period should be short—no more than five business days), do not tell other candidates in the queue that an offer has been made because if the offer is turned down, you can move forward without having the candidates feel as though they are second-choice candidates.

Interviewing Questions

It is crucial for you to be aware of the types of questions you absolutely can *not* ask during an interview. Federal guidelines are set up in such a way that disallows you from asking *any* questions that are not specifically based on bona fide occupational qualifications. This means that if the question does not match the candidate's skills with the position's qualifications, you may not ask it. Are there some gray areas? Of course, but if in doubt, do not ask the question. It will save you a lot of heartache and potential lawsuits. As a rule of thumb, always consider the following when developing questions for an interview:

- ▸ Develop only questions that will help you to determine if the candidate will be successful in the position for which he or she is interviewing.

- ▸ If at all possible, try to ask the same types of questions of the candidates interviewing for the same position. This helps to demonstrate that you have been fair and consistent in all of your interviews. ⁄

POINT TO REMEMBER!

If you want keep out of trouble and stay on the correct side of the law, just remember that if the question does not have anything to do with the specific position as well as the candidate's ability to perform the tasks required of that position, DO NOT ASK THE QUESTION! Please be advised that this is not worded in such strong language to scare or make the interviewer nervous. After a while, the interviewer will be able to do successful interviews as second nature. It is simply a matter of starting off on the right foot and forming good and legal habits.

Now let's examine the good questions and the bad questions.

No-Nos

You should never ask questions that have nothing to do with a candidate's ability to perform the function of the position for which you are interviewing. The guidelines vary from state to state, so you are better to steer clear of every one of the following questions. Doing so will save you a lot of trouble.

- How old are you?

- Are you pregnant or plan to be?

- Have you ever been arrested?

- Are you against abortion or pro choice?

- Are you planning to get married?

- Where were you born?

In general, do not ask any questions related to race, religion, age, politics, or sexual orientation. The list of questions you cannot ask is endless, so be sure to stick to the ones you *can* ask. As it should be, questions you ask during the interview should be specific to the position, its responsibilities, and the candidate's ability to function in that position. Finally, beware of methods you may consciously or unconsciously use to get answers to the no-no questions. Avoid these:

- Instead of directly asking a question that is inappropriate, you end up saying, "This is a great place to work for us baby boomers. I am 44 years old." Then you wait for a reaction. The candidate will often offer a comment to avoid the awkward silence. This is a no-no.

▸ You move away from a formal interview style and take on the "you can tell me anything" conversational style in the quest to befriend the candidate. This is a no-no.

It is in your best interest to do neither of these things. It shows a lack of integrity and professionalism, and compromises the interviewing process. An interview should be formal, documentable, and structured. You may interview many people in your career, but asking one inappropriate question could end it. A candidate who does not get the job might decide you were prejudiced based on one single question you asked. This happens every day. Don't let it happen to you.

Questions You Can Ask

Questions you can ask come in two categories—the technical and the non-technical. The definition of a technical question is a simple one. It should pertain only to the specific requirements of the position as specified on the position profile. The non-technical question is more general in nature and is designed to ascertain the attitudes and thought processes of a candidate, not to determine what a candidate knows. Remember the golden rule: Hire for attitude, train for skills—not the other way around. Over the years, I have developed a series of my own questions that are open-ended, thought-provoking, and help to add insight into the qualities and overall appropriateness of a candidate. Examples:

▸ What is the most significant contribution you made in your last position? How did it positively impact the organization?

▸ How do you set your priorities and manage your time? How many productive minutes do you get out of an hour? Why?

▸ What are the three most tangible skills you can bring to this organization?

▸ How can you support this organization's goals?

▸ What do you see as the difference between management and leadership? When is each applied?

▸ How can we help you to grow?

▸ How can we support you to be successful?

▸ What are you lacking that would otherwise make you a "10"?

▶ Why are you leaving your current position? How long did you work there before you realized you needed to make a change?

▶ How do you manage pressure and conflict within your group?

▶ How do you form and maintain relationships within the organization?

▶ Politics exist in all organizations. How do you get the organization and the people in it to do what is right? How do you determine what the right thing to do is?

Sample Questions

I know that many interviewers like to have the traditional war chest of questions at their disposal. The following 50 questions come from www.quintcareers.com/interview_questions.html. (I have adapted them slightly for my taste.) These questions are very useful when used in the right context for the candidate you are interviewing.

1. What are your long-range and short-range goals and objectives?

2. What specific goals, other than those related to your occupation, have you established for yourself for the next ten years?

3. What do you see yourself doing five years from now? Ten years from now?

4. What do you really want to do in life?

5. What are your long-range career objectives?

6. How do you plan to achieve your career goals?

7. What are the most important rewards you expect in your business career?

8. What do you expect to be earning in five years?

9. Why did you choose the career for which you are preparing?

10. Which is more important to you, the money or the type of job?

11. What do you consider to be your greatest strengths and weaknesses?

12. How would you describe yourself?

13. How do you think a friend or professor who knows you well would describe you?

14. What motivates you to put forth your greatest effort?

15. How has your college experience prepared you for a business career?

16. Why should I hire you?

17. What qualifications do you have that make you think you will be successful in business?

18. How do you determine or evaluate success?

19. What do you think it takes to be successful in a company like ours?

20. In what ways do you think you can make a contribution to our company?

21. What qualities should a successful manager possess?

22. Describe the relationship that should exist between a supervisor and those reporting to him or her.

23. What two or three accomplishments have given you the most satisfaction? Why?

24. Describe your most rewarding college experience.

25. If you were hiring a new graduate for this position, what qualities would you look for?

26. Why did you select your college or university?

27. What led you to choose your field or major of study?

28. What college subject did you like best? Why?

29. What college subject did you like least? Why?

30. If you could do so, how would you have changed your plan of study? Why?

31. What changes would you make in your college or university? Why?

32. Do you have plans for continued study? An advanced degree?

33. Do you think your grades are indicative of your academic achievement?

34. What have you learned or gained from participating in extra-curricular activities?

35. In what kind of work environment are you most comfortable?

36. How well do you work under pressure? How do you manage your work under pressure?

37. In what part-time or summer jobs have you been most interested? Why?

38. How would you describe what would have been the ideal job for you following graduation?

39. Why did you decide to seek a position in this company?

40. What do you know about our company?

41. What two or three things are most important to you in your job?

42. Are you seeking employment in a company of a certain size? Why?

43. What criteria are you using to evaluate the company for which you hope to work?

44. Do you have a geographic preference? Why?

45. Are you willing to relocate? Does relocating bother you?

46. Are you willing to travel?

47. Are you willing to spend at least six months as a trainee?

48. Why do you think you might like to live in the community in which our company is located?

49. What major problem have you encountered and how did you deal with it?

50. What have you learned from your mistakes?

There are abundant resources on interviewing theories and interview questions. However, you do not have to become an expert. My goal is to enlighten you sufficiently so that you become astute enough to ask the right questions, wise enough to make the right decisions, and understand the significance of an effective interview process in building a flourishing business, one person at a time.

4

The Decision to Hire

To hire or not to hire. That is the question (with apologies to William Shakespeare), and timing is often the answer. The offer is all that stands between the candidate going away and the candidate becoming an employee. Sooner is often much better than later because time can kill a deal.

The hiring process is something akin to dancing. It has an energized rhythm and flow that should be followed until its logical conclusion. Getting the candidate energized about joining your company is essential to making a hire, especially if you are competing with other companies for the same candidate. However, excitement has a shelf life, and if you let too much time go by, the candidate will lose that excitement and may lose interest altogether. To prevent this from happening, always let the candidate know *what* the next step in the process will be and *when* it will take place. (Give yourself a day or two leeway to avoid disappointing the candidate.) Also, if the hiring process is to be put on hold (e.g., a reorganization or a hiring freeze), tell the candidate right away. Although your candidate may be disappointed, he will appreciate being informed and will respect you (and your organization) for doing so. If left in the dark, your candidate will feel strung along and believe he has wasted his time with you and your organization.

Let's recap. At this point in the game, you should already have done the following:

- ▶ Followed the planning steps outlined in Chapter 1—laid the foundation for an effective, well-thought-out hiring process.

- ▶ Examined and selected all of the candidate generation options that meet your needs, as outlined in Chapter 2.

- ▶ Reviewed the material in Chapter 3 to help you prepare for the interviewing process. It is important to feel comfortable about conducting solid interviews. If it helps, think about it as conducting a meeting instead of an interview. It may relieve you of some of the stress.

The Offer

Making an offer is always a bit daunting because there is so much that is unknown. Namely, the candidate. True, you have interviewed (hopefully, more than once) and checked references. So, the decision should be relatively easy, no? Well, I know it's not. Experience has taught me a great deal about everything you should look for *and* look out for before making that final offer. Here are some of the lessons I have learned from years of hiring.

The Offer Letter

Offer letters can vary significantly from company to company, state to state, and one lawyer's opinion to another. Figure 4-1 shows a generic sample letter you may want to consider using as a guide, but your employment attorney should review it (or any other type of letter you use) to check for cracks, loopholes, or troublesome wording. It will be money well spent.

The High Cost of Making a Bad Hire

The sad truth is, sooner or later, we all make a bad hire. We might have interviewed poorly, hired under extreme pressure, failed to check references, or simply been the victim of any number of problems or difficult situations. This is the reality of business. If you've made a bad hire, you probably noticed problems in one of the following areas:

- ▶ Work performance
- ▶ Ability to form and manage relationships
- ▶ Content/technical knowledge
- ▶ Ability to manage time
- ▶ Ability to set priorities
- ▶ Ability to assimilate into the company
- ▶ Work ethic
- ▶ Personal problems

Candidates can fail to meet your expectations for a number of reasons, and the experiences can be painful and frustrating. However, you can make the most out of each circumstance by learning from each situation. Start by meeting with your employee and developing plans

July 21, 2001
Joe Smith
82 Elm Ridge Road
Stow, MA 01775

Dear Joe,

I am pleased to offer you the opportunity to join Technology Innovators as Director of Technology Services, reporting to Roger Sloan, CIO.

You will be compensated at the bi-weekly rate of $2,692.31 ($70,000 annualized) and will be paid a signing bonus of $5,000.00, which will be paid in two equal parts. The first payment will be paid at the end of the first pay period after you have been employed by Technology Innovators for thirty (30) days. The second payment will be paid to you after you have been employed by Technology Innovators for sixty (60) days.

In addition to your base and signing bonus, management will recommend at the first Board of Directors meeting subsequent to your start date that you be granted an option to purchase 2,500 shares of Technology Innovators Common Stock. This option will have an exercise price equal to the closing price on the date of grant and will vest over four years, with 6.25% vesting each quarter from the date of grant.

You will also be eligible for full benefits in accordance with Technology Innovators company policy. A summary of these benefits is enclosed for your review.

It should be noted that as a condition of employment, you will be required to sign an agreement that addresses the issues of confidentiality, conflicts of interest, non-competition, and patent assignments. Please sign and return this form along with the original signed offer letter in the enclosed envelope. Additionally, on your first day of employment, you will be required to provide the Company documentary evidence of your identity and eligibility for employment in the United States to satisfy the requirements of Employment Eligibility Verification (Form I-9) as required by Federal law. Enclosed is a copy of INS Form I-9, which must be returned with the original signed offer letter in the enclosed envelope. Failure to submit the required documents within the time requested will result in our having to terminate your employment.

Joe, we know that you have a lot to contribute to Technology Innovators and that you will be provided with an exciting, rewarding, and challenging career opportunity. We look forward to your acceptance of our offer and are enthusiastic about you becoming an important member of our team.

Sincerely,
Howard Adamsky
Director of Human Resources

I accept your offer as outlined above and will begin employment on _____.

Signature_____

Date _____

This offer is valid through July 26, 2001.
Upon acceptance, please return your signed offer letter, INS Form I-9, and the Invention and Non-Disclosure Agreement.

Figure 4-1: The offer letter

for improvement. But realize there will be times when nothing will make things better. Don't beat yourself up over it; we've all been there. The best thing you can do is to make sure you conduct an exit interview with the employee to find out what went wrong. Exit interviews aren't always fun, but at least you have the opportunity for open and honest communication, and to receive feedback regarding the candidate's opinion about what went wrong. After the exit interview, do a postmortem to see if the organization can learn from its mistake. This is such an important step that many organizations fail to take. Learning from bad hiring experiences can help prevent or eliminate the problems that often plague organizations:

- ▶ Wasted time

- ▶ Wasted money

- ▶ Wasted energy

- ▶ Wasted opportunity to have hired a better candidate

- ▶ Having to repeat the entire hiring process

- ▶ Work delays and missed schedules

- ▶ Poor reputation among competitors and peers

- ▶ Low morale

- ▶ Frequent turnover

Because there is no guarantee of a "sure thing," all you can do is develop a sound hiring plan, stick with it, use your best judgment, orient the candidate to your company and its objectives, communicate your goals effectively, monitor the candidate's progress, support the candidate's efforts, and hope for the best. If this sounds like an oversimplification for success, it is. But applying these steps and strategies consistently will give you an advantage over most companies out there. Lastly, don't be unrealistic by expecting 100 percent success. This is the way you set up a new employee for failure. If you have such high expectations, you will not be prepared to offer the guidance and support your new employee will need.

What Experience Has Taught Me

My vision is to create a better company by employing a better, more effective workforce. By making good hires and retaining good employees, you have the opportunity to move away from the norm toward incredible productivity—to be considered among not only the very best within your industry but within every industry. Corporate greatness is universally praised, collectively admired, and constantly sought after. To achieve this is both realistic and attainable. I would not have written this book otherwise. The hiring recommendations and advice I am about to give you in these sections are those I live by and hold dear. They are intertwined inexorably with my values and are central to achieving my vision. I believe wholeheartedly that they are fundamental toward achieving what Jim Mullen calls corporate "greatness," which is vastly different from the norm—corporate "bigness."

Hire People Who Are Smarter than You

Do not be concerned that someone coming into the organization might take your job because he or she is perceived as being smarter. If this way of thinking is built into the culture of your organization, over time, your company will become staffed with an increasingly marginal workforce that will require more and more people to do less and less work. This can impair your company's ability to compete in the long term. Bob Griffin, president and CEO of eMotion (www.eMotion.com), a Global Leader in Digital Media Management®, says, "The most important thing in hiring is to remember 'A' players attract other 'A' players." Success breeds success. However, not heeding Bob's advice could result in your company being filled with "C" players. There is very little else more debilitating to a company than the erosion of what was once its great workforce.

There Is No "Perfect" Candidate

Just as there is no absolute perfect job or perfect employee, there can be no perfect candidate. We dream of sorting through hundreds of résumés, interviewing scores of candidates, bringing in a select few for second interviews, feeling as though we are getting closer to that perfect candidate who will be approved by all. It never quite happens that way, of course. And if your hiring process gets stunted because of your reluctance to hire until you find this perfect candidate, you are liable to do more damage than good to your organization. No, there are no *perfect* candidates, but there are *great* candidates who can and will get the job done. If you follow your hiring and interviewing procedures, represent the position clearly and your company honestly, you stand an excellent chance of making a good hiring decision.

Degrees Are Not a Guarantee of Success

Degrees are a good measure of a person's level of education, but not necessarily a guarantee that he or she will be a better employee than a person with no degree. I am a student of behavior and workplace dynamics, and have made analyzing why people succeed and fail something of a second career. I believe that EQ (Emotional Quotient) is far more valuable than IQ (Intellectual Quotient) because failure in the workplace is most often due to lack of skills in dealing with complex relationships and interactions rather than in less-than-optimum intellect. I have not seen a strong correlation between advanced degrees and superhuman productivity and/or creativity in the workplace. I am not trying to knock the advanced degree holder. I just want to caution you from thinking that a degree is a guarantee of success. You don't want to become an organization that turns into a think tank, where much time is spent studying a problem instead of fixing it. Speed to market can mean the difference between success and failure. Very often, the fast-paced world of technology requires us to get 80 percent of the facts and make our move from there. Just be sure you look at the whole picture of a candidate, not just educational level.

Hire People Who Know How to Set Priorities

I am constantly amazed at how productive some people are and how others don't seem to get anything done within the same amount of time. It all comes down to being able to complete assigned work by knowing how to set priorities and manage time. What I mean by time management, of course, is one's ability to manage oneself within a given timeframe. Setting priorities is undeniably linked to time management—those who are good at one are good at the other. Setting priorities is nothing more than putting first things first—evaluating objectives and attending to the more pressing items before the less pressing items. I have read many books on interviewing that list 15 or 20 of the best and most revealing questions one can ask in an interview. Strangely, not one of them includes a question related to prioritization and time management. We seem to spend so much time assessing whether a candidate can do the job that we overlook whether the candidate *will* do the job. Remember these interview questions from Chapter 3:

> How do you set your priorities and manage your time? How many productive minutes do you get out of an hour? Why?

Very few interviewers ask these questions and it is critical to do so. Often, these questions will catch an interviewee off guard, so it presents a good opportunity for the candidate to analyze his or her own productivity and how priorities are established. There is really no right or wrong answer to this question. But, beware of the candidates who tell you they always work 12-hour days and on the weekends in order to get the job done. This gives no indication of a person's ability to set priorities or manage time. What you are looking for is some sense of understanding that setting priorities (and knowing how to be flexible) is necessary for achieving objectives.

You and Your Interview Team Do Not Have to Agree

Over the last few years I have noticed an interesting trend: In order to ensure you hire a good candidate, add more people to the interview team. This seems logical on the surface, but there is no correlation between the number of interviewers and a successful hiring decision. I once worked with a client who wanted fourteen engineers to interview one candidate. These engineers complained to me that they interviewed endlessly and never hired anyone. (Also, candidates ended up exhausted and lost enthusiasm for the position.) One of my recommendations was to streamline the process with group interviews, which reduced the interview time by two-thirds. Hires also tripled. Why? Because I also made it clear that it is not necessary for everyone to agree on a candidate in order to arrive at a hiring decision. There are two exceptions, however:

- ▶ If one of the dissenting votes is from the hiring manager.

- ▶ If at least one member of the team absolutely, unequivocally cannot or will not agree to hire the candidate.

It is perfectly acceptable for members of the interview team to disagree with the majority. It shows that there is a balance of diverse perspectives, and that there is no fear of voicing an opinion, even when it is in opposition to the group. Who knows…perhaps what one person says could be exactly what the majority is thinking. Take the time to examine and understand the concerns.

Should any one interviewer always have the veto power? No. You will lose valuable time and potential candidates. However, never bully the naysayer into agreeing with you. This will damage the group dynamics and discourage honest discourse.

Hire Candidates Who Value the Customer

No employee, in any position, should assume that it's not necessary to value the customer. Even if you do not interact with the customers, you must have an appreciation for them. A negative attitude toward clients will affect the health of the organization. Like the flu, attitudes are contagious. Your customers make a conscientious decision regarding where they spend their dollars. The cash register is the voting booth. No recounts. No Supreme Court decisions. In the early 1980s, the Chrysler Corporation nearly went out of business because of the power of the customer. The company wasn't producing the types of cars that people wanted or were satisfied with. I don't care who you are, what you make, or how much money you have—if a giant like Chrysler can almost slide into oblivion, your company can, too. If your employees do not appreciate your customers, your customers will go elsewhere. Winning clients back is very difficult. We say that we are customer driven. We say that the customer is king. How true is it for your company? Is it just a marketing slogan or is it management's edict? Ensure the health of your organization by hiring candidates who know the value of the customer.

An Example of Valuing the Customer

A major hotel chain teaches its employees that once a customer communicates to them about a problem, they own that problem. If it is not something they can fix, it is their responsibility to find someone who can. This same hotel chain strongly discourages its employees from pointing in order to direct a customer to a location. They are instead taught to escort the customer—to the pool, the restaurant, etc. This level of service has catapulted them to the top of the hospitality business. I can assure you that as their frequent customer, I feel valued when I am their guest.

Hire for the Future

Granted, this is not easy to do. So many variables and endless market shifts make predicting your future needs extremely difficult. Still, we have the responsibility to do what seems to make the most long-term business sense. Look for candidates who are willing and able to grow with the company over the next few years. If you have projections for significant changes or the need for new skills, look for candidates who have demonstrated the abilities you'll be needing. Obviously, the best way to determine whether someone will be capable of fulfilling your needs is to see whether he or she demonstrated the ability in the past. Look for candidates who have moved into positions of increasing responsibility. Ask questions during the interview about how successful they were in the various jobs. Many companies go through "need cycles," the need to call upon different skills as products move from one stage of production to the next. Pay attention to your company's need cycles. Do not overlook a potential hire even if you do not have an immediate need for him. His skills may be in demand sooner than you think.

Hire People Who Think Differently (from You)

If you hire in your own image, you will end up with people who think as you do, see the world as you do, and act as you do. You may wonder what is wrong with this picture. Well, you want to be challenged by new, different, and innovative ideas. As a result, your company will grow and so will you. It is through this growth that greatness emerges. Clearly, certain factors should be in alignment: values, integrity, and communication skills. But there are many ways to conduct business and many ways to recognize and respond to challenges and opportunities. If you find people who see the world differently, have the foresight to bring them into the organization. You will be well on your way to developing a team that values diversity and encourages ingenuity.

Ask the Ultimate Open-Ended Question

In the final stages of the interview process, the candidates usually have a pretty good feel for the position. They know about the company, where they will fit into the organization, and what is expected of them. The company is familiar with the candidate's skills and track record, and is comfortable with the prospects. It is at this point I usually ask the one question that hasn't been asked thus far, the ultimate open-ended question: "What exactly do you want to do?" I don't ask "What exactly do you want to do at this company?" or "What exactly do you want to do in this position?" I do not want to narrow the scope of the candidate's answer. Try to make all of your important interviewing questions open-ended. You will gain more information to share with others in the decision-making process.

- ▶ Open-ended questions require the candidates to come up with explanations. These questions tend to be the best types for interviews because they enable you to get the most information from the candidate.

- ▶ Closed questions are answered with either a "yes" or "no," (e.g., "Did you manage any engineers in your previous position?"). The answers provide very little insight into the candidate.

You may be surprised to find that many people actually do not want to do what they are being hired to do. I always hope, when I ask the question, that the answer is in alignment with the requirements of the actual position. Unfortunately, this isn't always the case. I once interviewed a candidate for a VP position in international consulting, and asked him what he wanted to do. He told me he wanted to revamp marketing. This was not the answer I was hoping to hear. In fact, it was not even close. Undaunted, I went on with my interview and asked him why, with a great track record in consulting, did he want to revamp marketing. He told me that consulting was not very exciting anymore, and required more travel and client interaction than he cared for. I sympathized with his feelings, but I had to pass on this candidate.

Worth Noting

Take the time, early on in the interview process, to find out what the candidate wants to do with his or her life. The sooner the better. It makes no sense to interview a candidate over a period of several weeks, and then find out that although you are interviewing him for a quality assurance position, he really wants to be a product manager. And if you hire someone, no matter how qualified, for a function he or she doesn't want to perform, you will risk low productivity and high turnover. Once that person does find a position that is the right fit, you will lose that employee.

However, even if your candidate's needs and the needs of a position aren't totally in alignment, this doesn't mean something can't be worked out. It is always easier to change an aspect of a position to suit a candidate than to try to change the candidate to suit the position. If you are hiring a networking person, at least be sure that this candidate wants to be doing some form of networking, and not wanting to become a Java developer on the first day at work. But remember, there is room for cross-training and growth within the company. Consider this:

Tell the candidate that career development is something the company supports. However, people are expected to commit to performing the function of the job for which they are hired for 12 to 18 months. (This expectation will help to weed out those who simply want to get their foot in the door.)

If you have candidates who are reluctant to make this commitment, you should be very careful about hiring them. Corporate objectives must be met before individual ambitions can be addressed.

Choose Candidates Who Take the Time to Look at Your Website

Everyone has a pet peeve. Mine is a candidate who has not taken the time to look at your company's website. You must question how serious the candidate is about the job and its responsibilities if he isn't serious about preparing for the interview. Such an attitude could be a bad sign of things to come. I never, ever go to see a potential client without reviewing, in detail, as much of the client's website as possible. I even go so far as to print out the splash page (the page containing specific links), and bring it with me. Do I do this to impress the client? Partially, but I do it primarily to be prepared. How can I have an intelligent conversation with potential clients if I have not taken the time to learn about who they are and what their companies do? How can a candidate prepare for a series of interviews (a situation where one is supposed to be at one's absolute best), and not have looked at the company's website? One of the first questions you might ask a candidate is what he or she thought of your company's website.

Hire for Attitude and Train for Skills

Attitude is everything. Employees with the right attitude who may not have all the skills you want can accomplish far more than employees with the wrong attitude and all the skills in the world. I have seen employees fail more for their attitude than for anything else. Attitude influences the way we see the world, and as a result, drives our actions and behavior. Look for candidates who see the glass half full, not half empty. Look for candidates who have a "can do" way of approaching problems, even if he or she is missing a skill or two. Training could take care of the missing skills within months. I understand that it is not necessarily easy to help an employee to acquire new skills, but it is much easier than trying to change an employee's bad attitude. One way to determine a candidate's attitude during the interview is to pay attention to how the candidate talks about his or her last company and the people he or she worked with.

Hire a Team Player Who Can Work Independently

Hiring "team players" is very much the "in" thing these days. In all the interviews you have been involved in, how many times have you heard "Do you consider yourself a team player? Can you give me some examples as to why you think of yourself as a team player?" True, as Les Brown, a world-class motivational speaker, says, "We do not win alone." However, with so much focus these days on being a team player, it is practically impossible to get someone to admit that he or she likes working independently.

I have a problem with what seems to be the universally accepted concept that if a person is perceived as a non-team player, he or she should not be hired. I can tell you from personal experience that some of the most productive team players are perfectly capable of working independently to get the job done. Every organization needs an employee who is willing to move ahead to complete a project while the rest of us are developing our Gantt charts and milestone schedules between endless meetings. These independent workers can be extraordinarily good contributors, and are less inclined to get bogged down in office politics or dither to obtain consensus to ensure everyone feels wonderful about everything. In essence, they get the job done. I know an organization cannot run well without team players, but I'm sure you have experienced watching a group of team players work for weeks toward a solution that never seems to get resolved. While you do want someone who works collaboratively with others, don't let that be your only requirement.

Writing This Book as an Example

Good, bad, or otherwise, I wrote this book independently (with the help of my editors, of course). If I had tried to write the book with a group of my peers (as I originally planned), I would still be writing it when I'm 80 years old. And there is no guarantee that it would have been one word better. One thing I find troubling about the team concept is when a group project fails, no one is willing to take responsibility or assign culpability for the problems. If this book bombs, I take full responsibility for it. And, hopefully, I will learn from the mistakes.

It is not only very important that people learn from their individual mistakes, but also from the collective or "team" mistakes. If no one is accountable for the problems, then you are left with a group of people who wring their hands and sigh, wondering what went wrong.

Pay Attention to Attitude

Do not assume you will be able to motivate an employee after he or she is hired. Instead, hire people who give you the impression that they are already internally motivated—people who have that "fire in the belly." Motivation comes from something deep inside, and trying to instill it in someone is an uphill battle. The people you hire need to be proactive. They need to have an attitude of ownership and responsibility, and to understand that the best way do get something done is to accept responsibility for the task and make it happen. It's what Les Brown calls "no matter what" people.

Beware of Candidates Who Name Only Peers and Subordinates as References

You do not want a candidate who names as references a peer who worked with him six years ago and one of his subordinates from his last job. References should, at a minimum, tell you about the following aspects of candidates:

- ▶ Strengths

- ▶ Weaknesses

- ▶ How they performed compared with others in similar positions

- ▶ Whether they met their goals

- ▶ What they were like to work with

- ▶ Whether they were difficult to manage

- ▶ Whether they would be rehired if given the opportunity

- ▶ How they managed relationships within the organization

- ▶ What their communication skills were like

- ▶ How they handle problems, failures, and frustrations

The candidate's peer would not be able to give you all the information you need because the peer would not have supervised or set the goals for the candidate. References need to be from the direct manager who has evaluated the work of the candidate. If your candidate hedges and tells you that his manager has left the company, this is a good time to test the candidate's problem-solving skills. Have him locate his former manager. It is the candidate's responsibility to provide you with management references.

Hire Managers Who Know How to Manage

If you are looking to hire managers, especially first line and project managers, you must ask the candidates how they manage (or lead) their employees. Talk about their management philosophies, results, problems, and successes. It is vital that you discuss these issues during the interview process. Learn how they reward and how they set goals with their employees. How do they deal with people who aren't meeting expectations? How would their style fit in with your organization? Make sure the candidate understands your management expectations. It is perfectly fine to hire people into management positions, even if they haven't managed before, as long as they are appropriately coached and mentored. Proper mentoring will help ensure the success of the new managers as well as the employees reporting to them.

References

"Bob, did you check Greenberg's references yet?"

"Yeah."

"Were they okay?"

"Yeah."

"You sure?"

"Yeah."

"Then send out the offer letter."

"Okay."

Of course the example just given is not the way you want to go about checking references. Proper reference checking is easier said than done. It is no wonder there are so many legal implications and thorny issues related to reference checking when you consider all that it entails.

What It Isn't

Let me tell you what reference checking is not. It is not calling a few cronies of the candidate you are interested in hiring, asking a few general questions, and hearing that the candidate is the best thing to come along since Honda's new Gold Wing. (Any riders out there? If so, email me.) Reference checking isn't making a few phone calls and going through the motions by asking the "right" questions. Doing so does not add value to your decision-making process.

My Philosophy

Successful hiring can be done without reference checking. That's my philosophy. This isn't to say I am opposed to reference checking. But what I am saying is that checking references isn't as indispensable to the hiring process as most people seem to think it is. Here's why.

Employees Can Fall Short Regardless of Whether You Check Their References

There are so many people whose references were checked thoroughly, hired, and then fired because they didn't meet expectations. And how many more employees are out there who have had their references checked, are doing poorly in their jobs, and haven't been fired yet?

Some managers hire candidates regardless of whether the references were poor. Sometimes the manager liked the candidate and chose to disregard the poor references. Often, the manager hires in desperation because of the need to fill the position quickly.

People Hire Without Checking References

This happens often at the senior levels of an organization. The VP of marketing might say to the VP of HR, "Send an offer out to this candidate for the director of marketing position." The HR VP asks about the references and the marketing VP responds, "No need. I worked with her ten years ago." Of course this reasoning isn't sound because the candidate is no longer the same person she was ten years ago. (Are you?)

Most People Do Not Know How to Check References Properly

Most reference checking is done so poorly that it is pointless to do it in the first place. People are not generally taught how to do references, nor do they assume the responsibility to do so when asked.

People Check References for the Wrong Reasons

Many people check references to cover their tracks (i.e., butts). We live in a culture where CYA is the name of the game. Most people live in fear that if an employee doesn't work out, someone will pay. The usual assumption is that if references had been checked, there wouldn't be a problem to contend with. The CYA concept results in the obligatory reference check, and not a constructive one that is designed to genuinely support the decision-making process.

Bad References Are Rare

You will rarely receive a bad reference for a candidate you're checking on for fear of legal action by the candidate. In my entire career, I have heard only two or three bad references for candidates I was checking on. Obviously, the candidates choose their references wisely, avoiding people who would portray them in a negative light.

An Important Point

The better you and your organization are in the hiring process, the less you will have to rely on the last-minute opinions of people. If you truly comprehend the objectives of your company, understand the position you are recruiting for, have a team that does a comprehensive interview, and takes the time to get to know the candidate's strengths, weaknesses, and accomplishments, you will be ahead of 90 percent of the interviewing world. This will allow you to make decisions based on solid information and a sound process, not on references of strangers.

I am in favor of checking references on candidates who are close to the offer stage. I recommend the hiring manager, a second manager, and one peer check the references. (The hiring manager should not check the peer reference—save that one for the peer.) The hiring manager needs to be one of the people checking the references, which is far more valuable than having HR recite what was said about the candidate. My recommendation is that if you have a solid, well-thought-out hiring process, then references need to be checked as a formality only. If you need to rely more heavily on those references, make them worth your time. Read the following sections to see how.

A Special Word for Managers

Always take the time to do one of the references yourself, no matter how busy you are. A 30- or 40-minute discussion on hiring, one manager to another, is a great investment whether you hire the candidate or not.

Potential Pitfalls and How to Deal with Them

Problem: Less-than-honest references.

Try as you might, there are times you cannot get the truth about a candidate (weaknesses, areas needing improvement) no matter how you ask the question. References are often fearful of saying anything bad about a candidate. (If I hear one more reference tell me that the candidate's only weakness is that he or she is too productive, I'll jump out of a window.)

SOLUTION: LOOK FOR ALIGNMENT BETWEEN WHAT THE CANDIDATE SAID AND WHAT THE REFERENCE SAYS.

Identify some key points you want the reference to address—very specific questions related to the responses the candidate gave you. By doing this, you can confirm the information your candidate provided. For example, if the candidate says that he led a team of six IT staffers in redesigning the existing organizational infrastructure and finished 28 percent under budget, ask the reference to tell you exactly what the candidate did related to that project. Do not give out any information. Be wary if the answers are vague or delivered in platitudes. Do not hesitate to pin down the reference and ask for specifics.

Problem: References can be sued for slander.

We live in a litigious society. If the reference is negative, the reference can be sued. If the individual giving the reference was not supposed to give out information because his company has a "no reference" policy, then the liability issue falls on that person alone.

SOLUTION: DROP THE PROBLEM IN THE CANDIDATE'S LAP.

Tell the candidate that the references he listed can't talk due to corporate policy, and have him provide you with other references. They may not be as recent as you might like, but unfortunately, you have no choice. However, if the references say that they can't give a reference due to corporate policy, call their HR department and confirm that policy. If HR says otherwise, it is possible that the references do not want to give a positive recommendation for your candidate. Ask the candidate why a reference is unwilling to talk. If ever there is a time for honesty, that time is now.

Problem: What if you make promises you can't keep?

If you tell a candidate that you will make an offer based on good references, and then the references turn out to be bad, what do you do? What do you tell the candidate? How do you proceed? You could be getting yourself into some pretty heavy legal issues, and you want to avoid a legal battle any way you can. Even if you win, you lose money and valuable time.

SOLUTION: JUDGMENT TIME FOR YOUR HIRING TEAM.
First of all, never promise a candidate anything, least of all a job based on references. No one ever said that you absolutely should not hire a candidate if he or she receives a bad reference. Nor should you have to hire a candidate for a favorable reference. Anyone can produce good references. As my friend Chas Douglis says, "Even Attila the Hun had three friends." References should be used as a barometer and a tool in the decision-making process, not as the final arbiter. If you receive a reference that leaves you uncomfortable, compare it with the other references. Look for threads of commonality. If you get three references that leave you uncomfortable, you are in trouble. Candidates wouldn't normally give references that will provide negative feedback. One would have to question the candidate's judgment here.

Final Thoughts

▶ Be careful about the questions you ask when checking references. The same rules apply to references that apply to interviewing. Ask only questions related to the position and the candidate's work.

▶ Be wary if all the references give you the same answers and stress the same things about a candidate. If the references sound rehearsed or identical, question them. Also, do not end a conversation with a reference if you are dissatisfied with the answers or if you need more support for your decision.

▶ Never tell a candidate that you will definitely make an offer if the references are good. If the references are poor, you have the problem of telling the candidate that the references were problematic. This puts you in an uncomfortable, sticky situation that could result in legal action.

▶ Do not allow any of your employees to give out references. Have all employees refer the caller to HR to confirm dates of employment and titles only. This is a good way to keep out of court.

▶ Put all information in writing as you check references. Be sure to date them. Do not wait and do it later or you will lose the flavor of the conversations and the details.

Figure 4-2 shows a sample reference sheet with examples of generic questions. Be sure to modify the questions to meet your needs.

Reference Check

Candidate: _____

Reference: _____

Position: _____

Interviewer: _____

General Questions

- What was your relationship with the candidate and how long have you known him/her?
- What were the candidate's job responsibilities?
- What were the candidate's strengths and how did they apply to the position?
- Did the candidate meet goals, objectives, and deadlines?
- Describe the candidate's communication skills and work ethic?
- What are some areas that you think the candidate needs to develop?
- Describe the candidate's leadership ability and/or management style?
- Would you rehire/work with the candidate again?
- How does the candidate get along with other employees?
- How does the candidate compare to others that you have seen in the same position?
- Is there anything else we should know about the candidate?
- Is the candidate a "perfect 10"? What is he/she lacking that prevents him/her from being one?

Figure 4-2: Sample reference sheet

Consider Using Contractors

There are times when it makes more sense to hire a contractor to handle a specific function. Depending on the particular needs of your organization and the timetable required, hiring contractors may be the way to go. The contractor market has grown significantly over the last ten years and shows no signs of slowing down, especially in the world of technology. It is estimated that the number of contractors, either outsourced or onsite, will continue to rise as new methodologies for harnessing and promoting technical talent are developed. First of all, you must understand the difference between a consultant and a contractor; the two should not be confused.

In his book *Million Dollar Consulting: The Professional's Guide to Growing a Practice*, Alan Weiss, Ph.D., (www.summitconsulting.com) describes a *consultant* as "someone who provides a specialized expertise, content, behavior, skill, or other resource to assist a client in improving the status quo. This intervention focuses on a specific client need."

Contractors have many of the same skill sets as people within your organization, and are brought in house for a period of time to meet a given demand. Very often they are an extra set of hands that simply supplement the workforce in times of great need. For example, if you are developing a new software application and are running behind schedule, you can bring in a group of contractors to augment your staff in order to meet your deadline. Contractors can be a great source of talent and can make a huge difference in employee workload and corporate productivity. Employers tend to use contractors for a host of different reasons:

They need resources. Very often companies use contractors to fill positions because they haven't been successful in making appropriate hires. It is fine if you use contractors as a short-term solution. You don't want to burn out your staff by asking them to do the work of more people, and hiring contractors can ease the tension and problems for a while. Do not wrongly assume that you can back off on your hiring efforts once you hire contractors. When you have your short-term fix, redouble your efforts to find and hire the candidates you need.

They are up against a tight time line. There are times when an organization must complete a project quickly or a number of deadlines crash in during a short period of time. Using contractors could be a good solution here. They come in for a defined project with clear deliverables and a defined period of time. And your staff doesn't have to work 80-hour weeks in order to complete the projects on time.

They need a person with a specific skill for a limited time. It makes no sense to hire a permanent employee because you need a temporary specific skill. If you are a software company that deals only in high-end Internet technology, but needs an Oracle DBA for a small feature of a product for six months (and will probably never need that skill again), hire a contractor. It makes no sense to hire a fulltime employee you won't need after the end of the project.

Tips on Contractors

I have dealt with many contractors over the years, and have gathered insights, strategies, and guidelines that have helped me.

▶ Never treat contractors like second-class citizens. They are there because you need them.

▶ It is reasonable to expect contractors to "hit the ground running," but do not have unreasonable expectations. You will need to invest some time in training and familiarizing them with the situation.

▶ Contracting prices are negotiable. There are many ways for contractors to be compensated.

▶ Hire contractors directly if you can. Agency markups can be over 45 percent.

▶ Contractors will generally charge less for long-term assignments.

▶ Define, in writing, the deliverables and timetable you expect. Be very specific, and leave nothing open to interpretation. Confirm that the contractor understands the expectations.

▶ Make the contractor a part of the team. If you take the crew out to lunch, include the contractor. This fosters good relationships at little cost.

▶ Do not expect contractors to do work for free by working them for longer hours without compensation.

▶ If the contractor is from an agency, do not make an offer of permanent employment unless it has been prearranged between all parties.

▶ Be sure that the contractor has the specific technical skill you are looking for prior to the hire. It's possible that the skills listed on the résumé are exaggerated.

▶ If the contractor is not meeting your expectations, deal with the problem quickly and fairly. If the problem can be resolved quickly, do so. If not, get another contractor.

▶ Communicate with the contractors on a daily basis, if only for a few minutes.

▶ Encourage contractors to yell for help as soon as it's needed.

▶ You have the best chance for success with a contractor if the project manager who supervises him or her is strong, even-handed, knowledgeable, and on top of all aspects of the project.

Hiring decisions are challenging because of the numerous variables—location, the labor market, business conditions, and corporate values. We will never get it right every time. However, if we strive to do better today than yesterday, we are headed in the right direction— toward the kind of progress that will make the ultimate difference.

5

Closing the Deal

I may be a consultant in my professional life but I am a sales person at heart. There is nothing that thrills me more than closing the deal. It doesn't even matter whose deal it might be. Just talking about it is enough for me. Someone once said, "Presidents may president and engineers may engineer, but if no one sells anything today, everyone can just stay home because nothing will really have happened." A society's economic engines depend on the revenue generated from the sales of goods and services. Sure the goods have to be invented, marketed, tested, and shipped, but if no one sells them, they just sit there like boat anchors. Making the sale—closing the deal—makes things happen. In the employment world, this means closing the deal by getting the candidate you want to join your company. It is essential that if you are part of the interviewing team, you do all you can to make this happen, especially if you have candidate contact. And do you know what closes the deal better than anything? Selling the company. There is nothing worse than losing your number-one candidate to your competition because you did not effectively sell the company. This chapter will focus on what you can do to help close the deal.

We Are All Sales People

Many people do not realize or see this. They say they are technologists, accountants, or auto mechanics who have never sold a thing. Not true. You do not have to have "salesperson" written on your business card to have sold something.

Consider this:

> Have you ever gone on a job interview and not "sold" yourself? We all have to promote ourselves continually in life in order to get or achieve what we want. As children, we tell mom that if we can get the toy, we will clean our room. (Sales and negotiation.) As students, if we do poorly on a test, we ask the teacher for an extra credit assignment so we can prove our competency in a different way. We convince our spouses on why we need a second motorcycle, our kids on why they need to stay away from drugs, and the powers that be on why we need a pool permit for the backyard. Our ability to negotiate, convince, and sell is the tool we use to get what we need and want in life.

You Must Sell the Candidate on Your Company (Over Your Competition)

Closing, in the employment world, means having the candidate choose *your* company over another. This is vital, especially if your candidate has three other offers and six more interviews to go. You should start selling the company with the very first phone call or email to your candidate; first impressions are crucial. In all selling situations, the best time is every time the opportunity arises. Remember to always use the soft sell—the candidate should not feel pressured. The best soft sell is your enthusiasm for the company.

Ten Ways to Sell Your Company

- ▶ Talk about the company culture—what makes it a comfortable, fun, and satisfying place to work.

- ▶ Tell the candidate what convinced you to join the company.

- ▶ Speak of the progress you have made, what you have learned, since joining the company.

- ▶ Give examples of some of the goals you have lined up for the next year and how you intend to achieve them.

▶ People often join a company because of the opportunity to work with specific people. Perhaps they are superstars or great managers. If applicable, talk about the people with whom you wanted to work, and what working with them is like for you.

▶ Speak honestly about what some of the organization's challenges might be and how the organization is overcoming them.

▶ Talk technology with the candidate. Spend time right at the computer and demonstrate how you do some of your work. Have the candidate join in; make it interactive. This is a great way to build relationships among technologists.

▶ Talk about the company's mission, goals, and operating principles.

▶ Talk about the company's reward system and how it applies to the candidate's position.

▶ Introduce your candidate to one of the corporate senior executives. Try to arrange for them to have a few minutes together.

The Basics

The first requirement for selling your company is that you must have something to sell. (For a refresher, review Chapter 3.) There are many kinds of companies out there. Some are great places to work, others not. The bad ones offer the candidate very little in terms of what they want and need for their career, lifestyle, and aspirations. The tips and advice in this chapter are predicated on your company having something to sell: It is an organization that can compete with others. (If this reality does not apply to your company, see Chapter 7.)

Before Beginning: Assign an Interview Lead

Most people do not seem to know what to do immediately following an interview. They may wander around, go back to work, or chat about the candidate. But there are critical things that need to be accomplished related to each interview. Think of interviewing as going for a ride in the car. Someone has to drive and be in charge of getting there. The role of the interview lead is threefold:

▶ To manage and drive the interviewing process for the position being filled.

▶ To work with the team to collectively determine whether the candidate goes on to the next step.

▶ To make sure the process does not stall. Decisions must not be put off, and the candidate must not fall through the cracks.

In most cases, the lead should be the hiring manager. Otherwise, it is best to choose a senior person as the lead on the hiring team. However, be sure to keep the hiring manager apprised of the status, at the same time communicating effectively with all interview team members.

After the First Interview

The interview team should meet and discuss every candidate after each interview. Everyone should come armed with the position profile (see Chapter 1), Candidate Assessment Sheet (see Chapter 3), and the candidate's résumé. You should discuss the interview immediately following the interview or at some point on the same day as the interview while your impressions are fresh. Discussions should focus on the candidate's strengths, weaknesses, and most importantly, questions the interviewers have related to the candidate's technical skills, character, and work ethic. You will be spending more waking hours with the co-workers you hire than the people you live with, so choose carefully. If someone drove you crazy, say so, even if you're not sure why. Use your assessment sheets to compare notes. If you rated a Java developer as a "1" and the rest of the team rated him a "3," this is the best time to find out why. Remember to keep in mind that the first interview is to determine which of the following two options you intend to take:

▶ Terminate the interviewing process and send out an SAI letter.

▶ Move on to a second interview.

The SAI letter should be sent as soon as possible. No one likes to be kept waiting, and the candidates need to get on with their search. If you're moving on to the second interview, it is important to make it different from the first interview.

Develop a Customized Interviewing Strategy for Each Candidate

If you handle the first interview correctly, you can plan the second interview to maximize the interviewers' efficiency. You do this by utilizing the information gathered from the first interview to shape the second one based on specific questions and concerns related to the first interview.

It is key to the success of the interview process to develop this game plan and assign different interviewers to focus on different areas of concern. It allows you to gather more of the specific information required to answer your concerns about a candidate. For example, if you are unsure about a candidate's ability to write CGI scripts, have your most knowledgeable team member question the candidate to determine his or her depth of knowledge (but never turn an interview into an interrogation). The second interview should never have the same interviewers asking the same questions. The second interview should be more purposeful, focused on areas of concern and geared toward a more serious look at the candidate's viability as an employee. This different focus adds real value to the second interview.

Talking Money

The second interview is the best time to handle some of the more delicate issues. Both money and benefits should be discussed here. Benefits can most easily be covered by a "Benefits at a Glance" handout. But money is "the big one," and because the second interview signals serious intent by both parties, it is the most appropriate time to discuss this topic.

Discussing money with a candidate is an essential element in closing the deal. It is also a potential land mine that can blow up before your very eyes. As a wise candidate once said to me, "Money is not the most important issue, but it is the best way to keep score." That, coupled with a good attitude, will help you achieve your hiring goals. I have worked deals where both parties were well apart in terms of cash compensation, but the right attitude and spirit of cooperation allowed us to close the deal. I have also seen situations where the opposing sides were so tied to their own inflexible expectations and egos, so concerned with positioning, that the deals fell through. Interestingly, the deals did not always fall through for much. Sometimes it amounted to the cost of a sandwich a day. What a tremendous waste of time, energy, and money! Here is a personal example: I once stood by and watched a great employment opportunity fall apart because the candidate wanted to make $70,000. It was psychologically important to him. The hiring manager did not want any new hires to make above $69,000. Yup. We lost the candidate for less than a thousand dollars. This should never have happened. The amount of time and effort to find a new candidate for that position took almost two months and cost an agency fee—all amounting to well above a thousand dollars. To add insult to injury, the manager wound up having to go to the mid $70,000s for the new player. A perfect example of short-term thinking at its worst, and everyone lost as a result of stubbornness and inflexibility. Talking money is something of an art. I have found it best to discuss cash compensation in a quiet conference room, when no one is hurried, hungry, or feeling any outside pressures that will interfere with a good, friendly conversation. Remember the following:

Money discussions should never be approached from an adversarial perspective. If you have come so far in the hiring process that you are beginning to put numbers together, neither party should be trying to take advantage of the other. The conversation should come from the perspective of developing a roadmap that will allow both sides to arrive at a solution that will be fair and acceptable.

Dealing with Candidates and Money: A Primer

Believe it or not, I have always wanted two things in life: A new Ferrari 250 and the chance to write a section in a book that deals with all of the things I know about closing the deal. I guess one out of two ain't bad. (I can't seem to sneak a 250 by my wife.) So here goes.

KNOW THE CANDIDATE'S CURRENT SALARY BEFORE THE INTERVIEW

If you are dealing with an agent, he or she should provide current salary information, in writing, to the hiring manager. The candidate's *current* compensation information needs to be complete and should cover the following:

- ▶ Base salary.

- ▶ Guaranteed bonuses and exactly how they are paid out.

- ▶ Incentive complementation and exactly how it is earned and paid out.

- ▶ Benefits.

- ▶ Stock options.

- ▶ When the candidate is to get his or her next review.

- ▶ Anything else that the candidate considers to be compensation, e.g., a car allowance, mass transit discount, or company paid parking. If a candidate has a company paid parking space that was negotiated for that candidate alone, you will have a cash compensation issue if the candidate does not want to pay for parking out of pocket.

You want the aforementioned information up front to avoid the following scenarios:

▶ You interview a candidate for a position that pays $60,000 per year and find out that the candidate is currently earning $85,000. It is a waste of your time and the candidate's time.

▶ You know only the candidate's base salary. You want to avoid the shock of getting to the offer stage and having the candidate say, "By the way, my bonus is another $20,000 per year."

NEVER DIVULGE THE SALARY RANGE

Do not tell a candidate that a position pays between $60,000 and $80,000. The candidate will always hear the high figure when the employer is realistically looking at the mid to lower part of the range. If you came to my house and wanted to buy my motorcycle, and I told you I was looking to get between $9,000 and $11,000, which number would you hear? What offer would you make? If a candidate asks about compensation, my standard response is the following:

The total compensation for the position you are interviewing for is more than competitive. If we move forward with an offer, before getting it out to you we will talk about specific numbers and do all that we can to create a total compensation package that you will find more than acceptable.

I understand that all candidates want a raise when changing positions. This is not unreasonable. But if a candidate is already at the top of your range, be sure that you let him or her know. For the right situation, many candidates will move laterally with the promise of a signing bonus or a six-month review with compensation based on performance.

NEVER LOW-BALL THE CANDIDATE

A low-ball offer is very upsetting to a candidate. Companies do this all the time and it never works. Even if the candidate accepts the job out of need, he will never forgive you and will leave as soon as a better offer comes along. Low-balling a candidate is short-term thinking. The Russians have a great saying: "They pretend to pay us and we pretend to work." Do not let this be the reality of your company. You can decide you do not want to make an offer, even at the last minute, but never low-ball the candidate. It lacks integrity and serves no purpose.

SET THE TONE

Candidates are not always the ones who bring up the compensation issue first. For the candidate or the organization, compensation can be a game or an issue of control. To alleviate the possibility of tension, I always tell the candidate the following:

> Let's not worry about the compensation issue. We can work out a situation that will be good for all concerned. I want to enter into the conversation with some degree of flexibility and a strong desire to make this happen. If we are committed to making something work, there is nothing that can stop us from doing just that.

Those few sentences have a calming effect on the candidate. It demonstrates that you are not going into the compensation phase wanting to get the candidate in the door as cheaply as possible. By setting the tone, you take control of the issue because you introduce reasonability and fairness into the equation, and it encourages the candidate to do the same.

THINK WIN-WIN

The candidate must feel that the offer is fair and competitive. If, for instance, the candidate is underpaid in his current position, it makes more long-term sense to bring him up to current value than to keep him underpaid to save a few thousand dollars. The loyalty you will earn and the rancor you will avoid will more than pay for itself. The company *and* the employee must come away feeling like winners. This is the best way to start a working relationship.

BE PREPARED TO PAY MORE

When was the last time you bought a new car? Did you pay more than you expected? When you find out about the options—a Bose sound system, heated seats—you begin to see the price tag rise. Hiring new employees is similar. Throughout my career, I can remember very few candidates who came with the price tag I wanted to pay. Sure, there were candidates available for my price, but after interviewing the more expensive candidates, I saw what the company could have for a few thousand dollars more. This phenomenon is what I call "the value to skill shift." Value to skill shift means you might have thought your corporate needs would be met by a certain price, but when you saw what another $5,000 or $7,000 would bring in, your perception of what you need shifted. This is very common. When we see a candidate who really impresses us, that candidate shifts our expectation level upward. We then compare every candidate, consciously or unconsciously, to that candidate. He or she becomes the standard. As Freud said, "There is nothing so difficult to give up as a pleasure experienced." This also applies to hiring. It is best to spend the extra money on a worthy candidate in order to invest in your company. If you don't, other companies will. And do you really want to see a choice candidate going to the competition?

CONSIDER SIGNING BONUSES

Signing bonuses can close the gap and help close the deal if you and the candidate are not seeing eye to eye in terms of salary. Signing bonuses are good for two reasons:

- ▸ They do not add to overhead because they are not part of the employee's compensation package.

- ▸ Signing bonuses are paid out only once, and therefore, do not throw departmental salary equity out of alignment. If you opt to give out a signing bonus, do not pay it out all at once. If you pay it in two installments, one 30 days and the next 60 days after the employee starts, you reduce your exposure to loss if the candidate suddenly quits. Do not try to make an agreement with a candidate that requires him to pay back the signing bonus if he leaves within a year. It is a waste of time and not worth the money.

CONSIDER A SIX-MONTH REVIEW

Another way to help seal the deal is to offer a one-time-only six-month review, accompanied by compensation. (After the six-month period, the review should return to the regular review cycle. In most organizations, the review is done annually.) Very often, the six-month review is offered in conjunction with a signing bonus. The combination is effective because candidates do not have to wait long to see a substantial increase in compensation.

Whenever possible, do not state a specific dollar amount. Doing so will set expectations for the employee, who could infer it as a promise. If pressed, tell the candidate that the precise amount will be based on performance as it relates to meeting specific objectives.

CONSIDER STOCK OPTIONS

With the decline of the dot.com world, stock options are less attractive than in the recent past. However, they still have meaning to those who have faith in a company and are not adverse to some degree of risk. Some companies give options to all employees, with more options going to upper management. Other companies give out options only to people in certain positions. Whatever is the case with your company, consider making stock options part of the hiring package if that is what it takes to hire a candidate. Keep in mind that when you offer options for a given position, you set a precedent. Future hires will expect you to do the same for them.

After the Second Interview

The basic process of the second interview is identical to the first: All interviewers should meet immediately following the interview to decide whether to move the candidate forward or terminate the process. If termination is the result, send out an SAI letter. If there are special circumstances related to the candidate or position, you might consider a phone call in addition to the SAI letter. The call is not easy to make, but it adds a nice touch. If the interviewers have had all of their questions answered and are satisfied with the candidate, it is time to move on to reference checking and the offer. (I recommend avoiding a third interview. It is better to keep the candidate for an entire day, in conjunction with the second interview, than to have him return for a third interview.)

Reference Checking

If reference checking is part of your process, do so. Request as references two recent former managers and a peer. The hiring manager should check at least one of the references. (Review Chapter 4 for more details.)

Making the Offer

This is the time to celebrate. It is the end result of a lot of hard work where you're nearing your primary objective—hiring the candidate.

That's the real prize. Let's look at some ideas to help you turn offers into acceptances.

Discuss the Offer Before You Make It

"Did Joe accept the offer?"

"I don't know. I didn't hear anything yet."

You will hear this exchange in most organizations. We make an offer, hold our breaths, and hope for the best. Rather than counting on anticipation and luck, let's discuss some strategies to help ensure a higher level of acceptances. First start by asking your candidate questions like the following:

▶ "Don, we are ready to move forward with an offer, and I would like to send it out tonight or tomorrow at the latest." (Always send the offer overnight or priority express, even if the candidate lives across the street. It adds importance and a bit of ceremony to the offer—the equivalent of serving it up on a silver platter. Also, in this way, you will know when the offer is received.) "I do not want to pressure you or ask for an acceptance right now, but the offer will be somewhere in the area of $69,000. Does this number approach the amount you are willing to accept?" If the candidate answers in the affirmative, repeat the candidate's response back to him.

▶ "Okay, so you are pleased with this offer and there is a good likelihood of your accepting it upon receipt?"

The purpose is to find out what the candidate is thinking and to get him in the frame of mind to accept the offer. If the candidate tells you that he has a high likelihood of accepting the offer, it makes it more difficult for him to reject it. In a sense, you have already laid the groundwork for an acceptance through your questions. (Naturally, if the candidate tells you there is a low likelihood of accepting the offer, it is your responsibility to find out why and do what is necessary to rectify the situation. Never make an offer that a candidate has told you he is likely to turn down.)

One of the very best things you can do is give the candidate a bit more money than the number you quoted. For example, if you told the candidate you are going to make an offer of approximately $69,000, make it $70,000. You should do this for two reasons:

▶ The candidate will be pleasantly surprised.

➤ You have broken a psychological barrier. Most people think in terms of $10,000 increments. For example, there is less of a difference psychologically between $93,500 and $94,500 than there is between $99,750 and the magic number of $100,000.

Put a Timetable on the Offer

Always put a closing date on an offer letter. The wording should be like the following:

This offer of employment is good until March 15, 2002, and will expire at midnight of that date.

Not including an end date on an offer letter allows the candidate to take as long as he likes to make a decision. This will slow the process dramatically. It is often debated how much time a candidate should be given to make a decision. In my opinion, one week, at most, seems reasonable. If my candidate can't make up his mind in a week, I begin to get nervous. A candidate must be able to demonstrate good decision-making skills and impress management, and accepting the offer in a timely manner shows off these skills.

Follow Up

After the offer has been sent, give the candidate 24 hours to review it. (There is nothing worse than calling a candidate and finding out the offer hasn't been received yet.) After the 24 hours, call the candidate and check whether he or she has signed the offer letter and sent it back. You are clearly putting the pressure on, but it's subtle, which is as it should be. If the candidate responds in the affirmative, congratulate him and then have the hiring manager call with congratulations as well. Set up a lunch with the candidate (and a few employees) within several days to discuss business. Doing so will get the candidate psychologically involved in the company. Do not meet the candidate at a restaurant, but rather, have the candidate meet you at your organization so he can begin to feel connected. Walk him around the departments and make a few introductions. Then at the lunch, you can begin building the working relationship, setting a solid foundation for success.

Using an Agency to Close the Deal

If the candidate you want to hire was found by an agency, use the agent to close the deal. The agent has a vested interest because he does not get paid if the deal falls through (unless he works for a retained search firm). Let's take a look at what you should know about agencies and some important aspects of dealing successfully with the agency world.

The Purpose of an Agency

For the most part, this book is geared toward IT professionals. They are handled by agencies more often than by retained search firms. However, some retained firms are opening up divisions to handle this agency-oriented work because it represents a new source of revenue. The purpose of an agency is to act as an outside representative for an organization to help attract and locate the talent you need through less costly means.

The Cost of Using an Agency

Agencies charge a percentage (currently around 25 percent) of the estimated first year's total compensation for a given position, and therefore tends to be expensive on the cost-per-hire scale. For example, if you plan to pay the new hire a salary of $70,000 with a bonus of $5,000, the total compensation will be $75,000. If the agency fee is 25 percent, you will owe the agency $18,750. If you can avoid using agencies, do so. My opinion is based solely on cost and not on the agency's ability to deliver. Rates, like everything else in life, are almost always negotiable, especially on multiple hires or if you are willing to give the agency an exclusive for a period of time. (An exclusive means you do not use a competing agency for a specific position for an agreed-upon time. This gives the agency the incentive to focus on your needs because it is not competing with any other agency in that timeframe.) Two weeks is typical for an exclusive. If you agree to an exclusive, stick to it. Most agencies tend to seek out many of the same candidates, so you can easily be found out if you break an agreement.

Agency Guarantees

There are several types of guarantees that agencies offer. Some guarantee continued employment of an employee for six months, others offer no guarantee. Do not use an agency that does not offer some sort of guarantee—a two- or three-month guarantee at a minimum. A typical guarantee is a 30-60-90 prorated guarantee: If a candidate leaves your organization before the 30th day, you receive a full refund; between the 31st and 60th day, a two-thirds refund; and between the

61st and 90th day, a one-third refund. Many agencies want you to agree to a replacement candidate, instead of cash, if a candidate does not work out. I am not opposed to this kind of arrangement, but keep in mind that you will be locked into working with the same agency and won't be able to go to a different agency, even if that other agency comes up with a better candidate for you. As a general rule, the longer the guarantee, the better protected your organization will be. Be sure to get the entire arrangement in writing, including a signature of one of the agency owners or principals, before you authorize permission to proceed. In some cases, agencies will tell you they already have the perfect candidate for you and you should interview him right away, before the agreement is executed. Resist the temptation to do this.

Ten Tips to Help You Work Effectively with Agencies

- ► Select very carefully. Agencies are your business partners. Do not work with anyone you do not trust or feel comfortable with.

- ► Have all of the agents meet with your hiring managers. Provide the agents with position profiles that are prioritized by need.

- ► Respond to agency submittals as quickly as possible. Agents do not get paid until the placement is made, and this means they are working for free until the placement. Show them the consideration they deserve for their efforts.

- ► If an agent does not submit good candidates, do not immediately write him off. Let him know what is lacking in the candidates. Be specific about your needs.

- ► On occasion, you may not "mesh" with an agency. In these cases, it is best to terminate the relationship.

- ► Never call a candidate—for any reason—until the agent gives you the green light to do so. Doing so will disturb the flow of the recruiting process and can confuse the candidate.

- ► If you have significant interest in hiring a candidate, work closely with that agent to plan the best way to close the deal. The agent can be a great help in supporting these efforts. Remind the agent that it is his responsibility to handle counteroffer issues with the candidate.

▸ Always tell the agent the truth. For example, I have been involved in hiring situations that were so disorganized and confused that I had to tell the agent I had no idea what was going on, but would get back to him as soon as I could. Agents will appreciate your candor, strengthening the relationship.

▸ Get back to the agents with candidate feedback as soon as possible. If you don't, agents can quickly lose interest and begin to focus on working with other companies. Agents don't necessarily need to hear a definitive answer on a candidate. But what they do request is not to be left in the dark. Any feedback is better than no feedback at all. If a candidate calls an agent requesting feedback, the agent wants to be able to give the candidate as much information as possible. Otherwise, he loses credibility and you will be to blame.

▸ Always honor the terms of the contract. Pay on time. And never try to renegotiate the terms of the contract after the candidate has been hired. Act with integrity at all times.

If You Do Not Use an Agent

If you do not use a third party to help you find a candidate, you are on your own to close a hiring deal. The following sections provide information to help ensure your success in closing the deal. Like it or not, you are the agent. You do not want any last-minute surprises like a candidate calling you on the Sunday before his first day at work, and saying, "You know, I've been rethinking your offer…"

Make Your Offer "Counteroffer Proof"

Your candidate is most likely to have second thoughts about your offer right after giving notice. His supervisor might put the pressure on or try to make him feel guilty about leaving. Anticipate this possibility by preparing the candidate for a counteroffer from his company. Tell the candidate you are confident he will not accept a counteroffer from his supervisor, and then outline the negatives of accepting one:

▸ Tell the candidate that people seldom leave their jobs for money only. They leave because of growth opportunities, working conditions, company culture, technology, the commute, career path. Let the candidate know that even if his company offers more money, it does not necessarily address all of the reasons he is leaving.

▶ Explain that staying for more money could affect his department's salary equity. This can cause a problem for management, who may not let the candidate forget it.

▶ Explain that if the candidate accepts a counteroffer of more money, he will see very little in future raises because he is already making more than other members of his department.

▶ Tell the candidate that even if he stays with his company, his manager may think him disloyal, and it will have a negative impact on his career and relationship with his company. His manager may think the candidate will try to leave again.

▶ Explain that accepting the counteroffer will make your offer null and void. And if after staying with his current job, he is still unhappy, there will be no place else for him to go.

▶ Have him consider the type of company he is currently working for—the disconnect between senior management and the general workforce. If an organization must experience resignations before it addresses the problems that exist, it is probably not a company with which he would want to entrust his future.

▶ Statistically, candidates who accept counteroffers leave the company within a year. And most never accept a counteroffer again after seeing it is a losing proposition.

PREPARE THE CANDIDATE

Make it be known that counteroffer pressure can be very subtle. Usually, management doesn't throw themselves at an employee's feet, crying "Please don't leave me!" Smart companies will leave an employee alone for a few days. This makes a candidate feel a bit insecure, hoping to be asked to stay. No one wants to turn in his resignation and not get asked to remain with the company. It is damaging to the ego and leaves the candidate feeling vulnerable. Smart companies may do any of the following:

▶ Take the candidate out to lunch or dinner with the people who mean the most to the candidate (mentors, racquetball partners, lunch buddies, and close peers).

▶ Choose someone who the candidate is very close to and team him or her up with the employee's manager. They have a heart-to-heart talk about appreciating the candidate, the future, new projects, and changes to come that will result in improvements.

▶ Finally, the company will offer the candidate more money.

Help the candidate prepare for such possibilities by telling him or her to respond to the counteroffer by saying, "I really do appreciate being valued but I have too much respect for myself and the company to even discuss a counteroffer." The candidate must let the company know that he has made a career decision, and ask to respect that decision so he can concentrate on finishing his work in a positive, productive, and professional manner.

It is impossible to list all the strategies a company will use to win back a prized candidate. I have personally been involved in vicious battles for candidates, and not winning all of them. If you understand the finer points of counteroffer pressure, and can explain them to your candidates, then you and they will be prepared for the psychological battle. Preparing the candidate well will make the counteroffer attack less effective. You will not always win. But careful preparation will help prevent your company from losing candidates. Be aware that from the time your candidate accepts your offer and gives notice, to his last day at work, he is in enemy territory. Keep in touch with him. Get him mentally involved in your company. Call to ask his opinions. Ask him to stop by and take a look at a catalogue to pick out his new furniture. Do anything that keeps the candidate looking at your company as his future and his current company as his past.

Down to the Wire

Airplane pilots say that flying is 90 percent boredom and 10 percent sheer terror. The sheer terror refers to the most dangerous and difficult parts of flying—takeoffs and landings. Takeoffs in the employment world are usually relatively straightforward and easy, but landing candidates can be a real adventure. To help you, I offer some solutions to common problems associated with closing the deal to "land" a candidate. Also keep in mind that if you can't close a deal under reasonable circumstances, it is best to agree to end the process entirely. This should be done in as fair, friendly, and upbeat a manner as possible, telling the candidate you are sorry things did not work out, but asking him or her to keep the door open for the future. Many times candidates who you can't land today end up coming back to close a deal 12 or

18 months later. Treat the candidate the way you would want to be treated under similar circumstances, and you will feel good about the outcome, whatever it may be. You want to become better at what you do, to learn from your mistakes, increase your closing ratio, accept what works, reject what doesn't, and create an organization that is better because you were there to make things happen.

Use Your Best Closer

Every company has its best closer, the "go to" person. The Big Gun (BG). The BG is the person you call on when you can't close a deal on a candidate you really need. Every company has a BG. He or she could be a division director, a senior executive, or a networking person—anyone close to the company who is enthusiastic and has a natural ability to nudge an undecided candidate over to your side. Use the BG if you need help. It's a sin to lose a candidate because you thought you could do it alone. Just as a company succeeds or fails on the collective strengths of all its employees, the successful closing of a candidate succeeds in much the same way. It is the responsibility of the team to close the candidate. I suggest the following:

- ▶ Give the Big Gun notice. Don't catch him or her by surprise unless you are facing a crisis and about to lose a deal.

- ▶ Tell the BG about the candidate and the position. Make sure the BG understands the issues that stand in the way of closing the candidate. Let the BG come up with the game plan.

- ▶ Introduce your candidate to the BG, stay for 30 seconds, and then disappear. There is no need to hang around. The BG will handle it from there.

The Candidate Accepts a Counteroffer

Stay calm and take a deep breath. There are many options here, and your response must be based on the hiring manager's philosophy on counteroffers. She could go after the candidate with guns blazing or refuse to deal with the candidate at all. If I were the hiring manager, I would be the "guns blazing" type. I do not like to lose. I don't support the "it's all for the best" attitude. If losing the candidate were acceptable, I wouldn't try so hard to make a winning offer to the candidate in the first place. Regardless of what you decide is the appropriate response, you must always follow one rule: Move fast. Very fast. Moving fast does not mean moving impulsively or being reactive. It means meeting with the hiring team, developing a plan, and implementing it as soon as possible. There is always a possibility of changing the candidate's mind, but if you wait too long, the candidate will snuggle back into his company. You must first call the candidate and find out what has transpired. Chat with the candidate, and if you then decide you will not pursue him further, that is your decision. I believe that in the struggle for good people, you never give up without at least some effort so that all your work was not in vain. If you intend to fight for your candidate, I suggest the following:

- ▸ Understand what you are getting yourself into. These types of tug of war can be tough, emotionally draining for everyone, and unpleasant. Be forewarned that it is rarely possible to turn around a counteroffer without the use of pressure. Use this pressure wisely and only when necessary, but do use it.

- ▸ Call the candidate and let him know you received his message about the counteroffer and try to arrange a meeting. Hold the meeting on your territory if possible, or if not, at a neutral location such as a restaurant for lunch or dinner.

- ▸ Remember to remain professional and pleasant at all times. Your best behavior is especially required at this time.

- ▸ If the candidate does not want to meet, try to arrange for a conference call in the evening after dinner.

- ▸ Finalize what you are willing to offer the candidate. More money? Title change? More responsibility, car allowance, the ability to telecommute on Fridays?

- ▸ Remember that the objective is to win the candidate, but not to win the candidate at any cost. Know where to draw the line and do not allow yourself to cross it.

- ▸ Ask the candidate why he accepted a counteroffer and what it will take to turn him around. Remind the candidate, very subtly, of the problems with accepting counteroffers.

- ▸ Set the candidate at ease and let him know this happens all of the time to employees whose skills are in demand. (It really does.) Act more in a consultative manner than in a sales manner. It will be difficult to win back the candidate if you do not know why he accepted the counteroffer, so be sure to let him talk for as long as he needs.

▶ At the appropriate time, say this to the candidate: "Don't you find it ironic that it took your resignation to make the company notice the problems you are experiencing? If you did not resign, do you think your manager would be doing all of this for you? Do you still want to work for an organization that waits for people to resign before making promises to change? In the long run, counteroffers are counterproductive and do not work."

Your best shot is saying something like the previous quote—sincere, truthful, and stated compassionately. If you still cannot convince the candidate to change his mind, you must determine whether continuing to pursue him will anger him. You do not want to use pressure that is inappropriate or unprofessional. If need be, part as friends and move on. Who is to say what will happen in six months? I always keep in touch, on a monthly basis, with candidates whom I've lost to counteroffers. Letting them know the door is still open is a good way to allow the candidates to accurately assess their situation and determine if they made the right decision.

INVOLVE A PRESIDENT OR CEO

Company presidents and CEOs are very busy, correct? Well, yes, but I have worked with many who can spare five minutes to phone a valued candidate in order to help close a deal. Five minutes is all it takes to do something so simple, and yet, so effective. Understand that an out-of-the-blue call in the evening, from the top honcho, just to say "I am aware of who you are, I am impressed with your background and really hope you join our winning team," sends a very powerful message. Anyone, including the CEO, should be able to find five minutes for a quick call to support the troops as they help to build the company. I am not suggesting that a president or CEO get involved in calling all candidates your team wishes to hire. But this type of action clearly demonstrates great business sense and clever marketing as it relates to hiring. If it makes sense in your judgment to have the CEO, president, or vice president lend a hand, ask for their help. Consider this another tool in your arsenal of closing candidates.

The Candidate Turns Down Your Original Offer

The candidate is, in my mind, not the final arbiter. A candidate turning you down can be the beginning of an interesting dialogue that will turn the candidate around. Call the candidate and arrange a meeting. Find out what went wrong and do whatever is reasonable and intelligent to fix it. Use the same philosophy that applies to the counteroffer—good judgment and the determination to win.

Handling the "Sore Loser" Phone Call

IT-oriented companies do not like to lose good employees. On rare occasions, you may get a phone call from your candidate's former organization, complaining that you "stole" their employee. This is patently absurd and should be handled in a polite and professional manner. If you should ever be on the receiving end of one of these calls, be gracious, let the person vent a bit, and use my standard response: "Candidates are not stolen. They make their own decisions based on what is best for their individual careers."

6

Retaining Your Employees

I was born in Brooklyn, New York, in the early 1950s in an area called Crown Heights. (Email me if you are from Brooklyn!) It was a great place to grow up, filled with homes of every conceivable type and style. Apartment houses and hotels were everywhere. From the outside, they tended to look the same, but the insides were quite different. In hotels, you never got to know the people in the room next to yours, but in apartments, people put down roots, and the relationships you forged with your neighbors could last a lifetime.

Companies are like hotels or apartment houses: The way you build your organization determines the type of establishment you end up with. If you work on retaining employees and create a positive environment where people can work efficiently and productively, your company will have an enriching, solid future that will prove itself in more ways than one. This sense of worth (not just in dollars), continuity, and connectedness will determine whether your company has a sense of permanency or is simply a place for people just passing through. Is your company a "hotel," where people learn what they can, make a contribution, and leave through the revolving door you have created? What kind of organization do you wish to build?

Let's examine the concept of retention and what it really means. Let's look at what you can do to build a strong foundation for your organization. But be forewarned. Working at retaining employees is hard work and takes constant commitment. Don't waste your time worrying about retention if you fall into any one of the following categories:

▶ Your company does not care about your people, the company culture, or the importance of building a business.

▸ Your company belongs to the "get rich quick" crowd. (There are very few that win in the long term.)

▸ Your company hires as fast as it can and focuses on an IPO in 18 months.

Do not look at retention as just another task to be checked off the to-do list. Retention is ongoing and driven by senior management's desire to hold onto great candidates and not lose them to the competition. If you and your company are committed to building a solid business, employee retention should be high on your list or priorities.

Company Culture

Culture is easy to define if you simply look it up in the dictionary, but difficult if you try to define it in the context of your workplace. Company culture is composed of elements, both seen and unseen, that make up the look, feel, and style of what the organization is all about— how it feels to be an employee of the organization. One of the most common questions candidates ask during interviews is "What is the culture like here?" The question seems simple enough, but the answer is not always easy to come by. Company culture is defined by each employee's perception. One person may see the company as laid back, supportive, and fun, but another might perceive it as authoritarian, heavy-handed, and controlling. Corporate leaders often try to set up a "comfortable" culture, but the attempts can be sabotaged by corporate or office politics, day-to-day business pressures, and workload. Great organizations work hard at building cultures that employees value because great cultures create the best workplaces. Organizations with a good, solid company culture all have the following characteristics in common:

▸ Open and honest communication

▸ Proactive management

▸ Emphasis on career development

▸ Strong leadership with demonstrated integrity

▸ Customer-focused employees

▸ Solution-driven employees

- ▶ Strong Human Resources support
- ▶ Solid values and a clear mission statement
- ▶ Fun
- ▶ Energy

If your organization is making a serious effort toward developing these concepts, it is well on its way to establishing a place that people respect and appreciate as a place where they want to work.

Defining Employee Retention

Over the last few years, organizations competing for top IT talent have observed the soaring cost per hire of prized candidates, and realized there must be a better way to run a company. A more cost-effective, time-efficient, and proactive way. (Some companies even reported cost per hires averaging almost $20,000 in the year 2000!) Retention—the ability to hold on to your prized employees for as long as possible—is the answer.

The cost per hire for many high-quality candidates has risen steadily over the last five to seven years. These types of candidates include

- ▶ Senior sales executives
- ▶ Marketing professionals
- ▶ Product managers
- ▶ Pre- and post-sales representatives
- ▶ Marketing communications professionals
- ▶ Corporate technology consultants

Why Employee Retention Is Important

The search for candidates eats away at departmental productivity. Let's face it. Attracting and hiring top-flight candidates is expensive and wrought with unexpected difficulty.

The solution, of course, is to put in place a strategy to retain your best employees. But first, you must identify your best in order to work to keep them. This is not as easy as it sounds, especially if your organization employs 500 or more people. Philosophically, employee retention is important because it is senseless to let good people leave your

organization. When they leave, they take intellectual property, relationships, investments (in both time and money), an occasional
employee or two, and a chunk of your future. From a more practical
standpoint, retention is important because

▶ Replacing good employees is extremely difficult.

▶ Training new employees is costly.

▶ Poor retention creates a "revolving door" culture within the
organization, lowering morale and confidence.

▶ Poor retention affects your customers. (No matter the type of
business you have, your customers develop relationships with
their contacts in your organization.)

▶ High turnover eats away at your organization's productivity,
ability to deliver, and overall efficiency, which affects customer
satisfaction.

Factors Affecting Employee Retention

First realize there is no magic wand, no single answer as to how to
retain your employees. Many factors that you cannot control affect
retention. Some of these include

▶ Shifting markets

▶ Demand for specific skills

▶ Business conditions

▶ Demographics

▶ Lifestyle changes

▶ Technology issues

▶ Trends in work/life decisions as employees' needs change

Retention is not affected so much by the things that you *do* as
a company as the things that you *are* as a company. Realizing this, to a
small degree, senior management has tried a great many things to create what they thought would be good for employee retention: Casual
Fridays (soon to be casual every day), flex time, telecommuting, and
food. Company-paid pizza lunches; wine, cheese, and nachos on Friday afternoons; cookies and prizes at meetings, and on and on and on.
But notice. These are things a company *does*, not what a company *is*.

A few of these changes have, in fact, resulted in some degree of employee retention. However, casual work days and pizza lunches only address surface issues and are mostly superficial. As a result, they will never affect retention in the long term. But, really. Would pizza lunches affect *your* decision to accept a better work opportunity? No. And most feel as you do. These types of changes are well-meaning, but not meaningful. If you really want to make a difference in your organization and improve your employee retention, read on.

Worth Noting

Beware of serving alcohol at company-sponsored events. It is a breeding ground for lawsuits and will cause great harm to your organization. Be observant of how much people drink. Treat alcohol with all of the seriousness that it requires and deserves.

17 Effective Ways to Retain Employees

First, it is crucial to develop a company and culture that address the changing needs of its growing workforce while, at the same time, remain true to the organization's operating principles and core values. Let's take a look at the essentials of company culture that will give you the best chance for success.

1. Hire Only the Best Candidates

The interviewers and those who make the final hiring decisions are the gatekeepers of an organization. They should be letting in only the cream of the crop—no compromises. This should be upper management's philosophy and yours. Having said this, you may now ask "How do I identify 'the best'?"

- They are capable of performing the job function at a consistently high level of competency after a reasonable learning curve.

- They want to work at your organization and do it with a positive attitude.

- They have a track record of success in a related field, or they have skills that are transferable.

- They are candidates who you thought were superior when measured against other candidates with similar skills and experience.

- They are candidates who you think will do well when measured against your best employees performing the same job function.

> ▸ They have a good attitude, communicate well, and genuinely wish to be a part of the team to support the organization's overall success.

Great people want to work with great people. They are influenced by each other and, over time, continue to improve. Mediocre employees hurt morale, productivity, and progress, making themselves and others lose faith in the system and the organization. You will never have the best company without the best people.

2. Work to Make Sure Employees Are Satisfied with Their Jobs

Create reasons for people to join your organization *and* to stay. See that people enjoy their jobs and the responsibilities they have. They must have a good understanding of how what they do supports the objectives of the organization. You must offer feedback so they know whether they are meeting expectations. Talk to your employees on a regular basis. Never assume things are rosy because you have not heard any different. By the time you hear bad news, things are probably far worse than you expect. These surprises are seldom positive. Especially be sure to communicate with new employees on a regular basis. Do not watch them "sink or swim." Set goals, coach, and make sure they succeed. I suggest a one-on-one with each new employee at least once a week. Do this for a few months to review progress and address concerns that arise both for the employee as well as the manager. In this way, you are being proactive rather than reactive and it allows you to catch small problems before they become major ones. Your employees will feel valued, motivated to do their best, and will take pride in being a part of a successful organization.

3. Let It Be Known—Your Organization Wants the Best

The organization needs to let its employees know that as a company, it is always on the lookout for exceptional talent and not just trying to fill open positions. Even if there is no open position, brilliance demands a place. If you locate a candidate who is clearly a "must have," make room for him or her. And most importantly, it is more effective to change a position to fit a person than the other way around. It speaks volumes about your organization's overall commitment to seeking excellence if you put this philosophy into practice.

4. Develop Your Employees

Great employees want to become even better. You can help by developing employees in the following ways:

▶ Develop a comprehensive career advancement program that offers training and creative career paths so employees can develop their skills and enhance their professional growth. Link professional growth to tangible rewards.

▶ Develop a mentoring/coaching program for all employees. Studies show that organizations with mentoring programs retain employees longer than organizations that do not because of the close relationships formed between mentors and employees. And, as an added bonus, you have more productive employees because they have been trained properly.

▶ Allow employees to move in different directions within the organization. People can be promoted, move laterally, or be assigned to special projects. This movement can be good for the organization and the employee because it promotes depth and understanding of the business. It allows the employee to view the workings of the organization from different angles.

▶ Always look within before you look outside to promote. Your current employees deserve to get first crack at new opportunities because they are the ones who have helped your organization succeed. In the past, most employees had to change companies to get promoted. Do not let this become a part of your culture. If you look to the outside for positions that can be filled internally, your employees will act in kind and look to the outside when they want to advance.

5. Treat Your Employees the Way They Want to Be Treated

This is according to Martin Levin, recruiting operations manager for the U.S. at Gentronics (an information and communication technology provider). This is very unlike the common notion that people should be treated the way *you* want to be treated. If you really think about it, this is a fundamentally flawed sentiment because not all people are like you and wouldn't necessarily want to be treated the way you would want. Every organization consists of all sorts and types of employees with different needs. Learn what those needs are and accommodate them as best you can. Remember that one size never really fits all when it comes to the delicate and temperamental aspects of dealing with people, their requests, ideas, and opinions. Think about these three points when interacting with your employees:

- ▶ People have a fundamental need to be heard and understood. Be a good listener. Look the person in the eye and try to make some type of connection.

- ▶ Follow up on all conversations. Let people know what your next step is and when you will be getting back to them. Then do exactly as you promised. You will gain great credibility within the organization and will become known as the person people can count on for results.

- ▶ Never leave people hanging. Nothing kills credibility faster than telling people you will get back to them and not doing it. People expect results. People expect answers. Be sure to provide them with some sort of answer even if the news is not what they want to hear.

6. Create Fun

People want to have fun. We all know that work is work—tiring, stressful, competitive, and demanding. All the more reason to create some fun in the workplace. And, of course, your sense of fun may not be the same as your employees', so do the following:

- ▶ Ask your employees what they want by conducting a survey, appointing a committee, or sending out emails.

- ▶ If your company is large, managers can and should ask their employees directly.

- ▶ Post announcements on your company's intranet.

- ▶ Do "paycheck stuffers" that request employees to write five things they want to see incorporated into the organization.

- ▶ Give out prizes to the person whose idea is selected (dinner for two, weekend getaway).

If you take the time and effort to ask, employees will expect you to act on their requests. Don't bother asking if you intend to do nothing.

You will create an undercurrent of resentment and your employees will see future attempts as meaningless. If for some reason you are unable to proceed with the requests, acknowledge your employees by informing them in a clear and concise manner so they understand the reasons behind your decision.

7. Get to Know Your Employees

This is not easy, especially if you are a Fortune 500 company. But is your company that large? If the answer is "no," take a few minutes to step into your employees' offices and ask a question or two about their projects. Get their opinions on industry trends. If you see pictures, ask how old their kids are. You want to care about your employees as people, not just as workers in your organization. Five minutes can be a great investment. I knew someone who worked in a mid-management position for a well-known technology company that employs well over 200,000 people. While on a visit to her location, the CEO stopped in and chatted with her for ten minutes about nothing much in particular. He then thanked her for her time. When she told me the story, she absolutely lit up. It clearly meant a lot to her. Another example is Norman Augustine, who was Chairman of Lockheed Martin (and a truly nice man). He used to go to the cafeteria at the Lockheed Martin corporate headquarters and randomly ask employees whether they minded that he eat with them. Perhaps this is why so many Lockheed Martin employees liked this man and why there is no shortage of 25-year veterans at that company.

8. Never Refer to Employees as "Bodies"

"When can we get some bodies in here?" How many times have you heard that (or said it yourself)? It is dehumanizing and condescending. It sets a bad tone and does nothing to endear you to the employees in your organization. Especially avoid using the term in the context of hiring.

9. Communicate Effectively

One of the complaints I hear most often from employees is the lack of communication from senior management and between departments. I just finished working with a client whose marketing and sales departments do not communicate with each other. Can you believe that? How does an organization exist if sales and marketing do not communicate? Set the tone at the senior management level and work on communication. Ensure that information is disseminated to the employees. Hold monthly meetings that include questions and answers. Make sure managers meet weekly with their staff. Use video-conferencing, if necessary. Communicate via newsletters. Foster open and honest communication. Use facilitators for difficult or non-existent communication. Give the bad news as well as the good. Make use of this tip from Toastmasters:

> When meeting with a group, first give out the good news, focusing on the positive. Then address the bad news. Do this with a positive, "can-do" attitude, presenting your solutions and asking for feedback. Finally, finish up with more good news, ending the meeting on a high note. This is also the time to acknowledge people or departments. (Always praise in public and criticize in private.)

Informed employees are dedicated, committed employees, so make outstanding communication your mission at all levels of the organization.

10. Make Sure Your Leaders Lead

If you are the CEO of your organization, this is for you. Your position is all about leadership, working with your team to set and execute the vision, and driving the process to achieve corporate objectives. Your staff is watching you very closely, and they have invested their careers, their futures, and their trust in your capable hands. Make sure you earn that trust. Lead with courage, conviction, and integrity. In his book *The Simple Art of Greatness*, author Jim Mullen says that your employees "pay little attention to the things that you say in your grand and gassy speeches." He is absolutely correct. Your people will listen to your speeches with half an ear, but they will watch you and evaluate your leadership skills very carefully. Perform in a manner that is inconsistent with the integrity spoken of in your operating principles, mission statement, and corporate philosophy and you will lose their respect. Worse, they will do as you do and behave as you behave.

Another characteristic of great leadership is knowing to communicate effectively on *all* issues, both good and bad. Do not assume you can keep your employees in the dark. They *will* find out. I can tell you from my experience of handling more than 20 clients, your staff will discover news with lightning speed. Unfortunately, because the news did not come from you, it is often twisted and out of sync with reality. It is said that managers want to be liked and leaders want to be respected. If, as a leader, you wish to be admired, act in a manner that deserves that honor. Admiration is earned. The companies that demonstrate genuine, forward-thinking leadership outweigh those that don't by a wide margin.

If you want your employees to stay, it should be your goal to create a company and culture that are a model of leadership that makes staying with the company far more sensible than leaving it. Lead well.

11. Pay Well

Compensation is extremely important: It buys all the things people need, and more to the point, it buys all the things people want. It reinforces people's sense of value and worth to the organization. And, obviously, no one wants to feel underpaid. Employees must feel good about their compensation package. Allowing good people with proven track records to leave the organization because of lack of compensation is unforgivable. Conduct salary surveys, consult with your human resources staff, and keep your ear to the ground to find out what the competition is paying. Do it now, proactively, before you are blindsided by one or more resignations. If you find that your employees are underpaid, look at industry norms, and make appropriate adjustments. This will send a loud and clear message to your people that you are taking care of them. They will feel valued.

Lastly, one more thing to keep in mind. Salary adjustments are just that—adjustments, not raises. If you find that an employee has been underpaid and you make the appropriate adjustment, do not look at this as a merit increase when review time rolls around. Do not confuse the two. If you do, your employee will not only be resentful, but will wind up behind the salary curve again and you will be right back where you started.

12. Fire People

I am aware of a disturbing reality. Employers do not want to fire poor performers. No, let me rephrase that. Employers may want to, and they might even plan to. But the problem is, they seldom do. Here are all the excuses:

- ▶ Fear of lawsuits
- ▶ Sympathy

- ▶ Lack of documentation

- ▶ Employee is not bad enough to be bad but not good enough to be good

- ▶ The "There, but for the grace of God go I" mentality

- ▶ Confrontation avoidance (though it need not be confrontational)

- ▶ Not knowing how to fire

- ▶ Hoping employee will become a better performer

- ▶ Personal relationships

These reasons are understandable. But, not firing a poor performer is bad for the good performers and bad for the organization. Firing people is a natural part of doing business and a part of your job as a manager or leader. Firing people is not necessarily bad. I think it was Harvey Mackay—author and syndicated columnist—who said. "It is not the people you fire who make your life miserable. It is the people you *don't* fire." A CEO once told me about the difficulty he was having with his vice president of marketing. I asked him what he had done to fix the problem, whether the employee understood her position, what the issues were, and how long the problems had been going on. Eighteen months! Eighteen months of unnecessary pain and loss of productivity. After looking at the problem from every angle, I gave him my advice: Fire her. (Fortunately, he had a year's worth of documentation.) When he did finally fire her, I was there to see it. I had never seen two happier people. She was relieved to end the pain and he was relieved it was over and could look for a replacement.

Here's something to keep in mind: If a person resigns and you jump for joy on hearing the news, perhaps you should have fired the person long ago. You may be doing him or her a favor. People are meant to succeed, not fail. Help those who are losing become the winners they were meant to be. Support their efforts to find another position. Do all you can to maintain their dignity, be sure the process is 100 percent legal, and offer a fair severance package.

I am not suggesting you go on a firing jag, but I do believe that firing people who are not performing will make your company a better place for all. You and the one you want to fire are not the only ones suffering. If you maintain the status quo, the co-workers suffer on two fronts—having to deal with problems caused by the poor performer and decreased faith in you as a leader. If you fire poor performers, you will be doing a good thing for the organization as well as the employee.

THE LEGAL SIDE OF FIRING

▶ Always consult with an employment lawyer or a human resources representative who specializes in employment law before you fire anyone.

▶ Never fire out of anger.

▶ Document the reasons for firing an employee (any problems, disputes, assignments missed, etc.). Be sure to keep all information in a folder. Lawyers call this "papering" your case.

▶ Make sure to discuss the problems with the employee and communicate, in writing, what your grievances are. Use clear language and specify examples. Document dates and how the employee's shortcomings caused problems. Provide a written statement with all information to the employee, and have him or her sign it. The signature line should be labeled "read and understood." An employee's signature does not indicate that he or she agrees with the information contained in the document.

▶ If the employee refuses to sign the document, simply write on the document that the employee refused to sign. Never pressure the employee to sign this document.

▶ Be consistent in how you treat all your employees. Do not fire an employee to make an example of him or her.

▶ Always fire the employee in his or her office with the door closed. Consider having a member of human resources or a neutral manager present to act as a witness to all that is said. Make the meeting short, and do not apologize. Let the employee talk, if necessary. Then leave and close the door, allowing the employee time to compose himself. If you are concerned about violence, inform the local police and get advice. It is better to err on the side of safety.

▶ It is seldom a good idea to allow the fired employee to remain in the workplace for a significant amount of time. Give him an hour or two to pack his belongings. If there is a lot of packing to do, agree to a time and arrange for a neutral party to help. (Friday evenings and Saturday mornings are often convenient and appropriate.)

▶ Never make the firing personal. If it is the end of a long war, do not act as though you have won.

HOW FIRING HELPS

▶ It demonstrates that you as a manager and leader did what was expected of you. People will respect you for doing it.

▶ It allows you to hire a successful replacement.

▶ It enables employees to associate and work with others they respect, admire, and value as significant contributors to the organization.

13. Conduct Exit Interviews

Exit interviews are as important as employment interviews and are invaluable to the organization. In an exit interview, the employee tends to be honest because he or she has no reason to lie or to embellish (as might be tempting in an employment interview). This brutal honesty can mean an unpleasant experience for you. Try to make it as relaxed as possible or have another more neutral manager from a different department conduct the interview. You will hear things in exit interviews that you may not want to hear, but need to hear. It is vital that you try to understand issues from the employee's perspective and give him or her the opportunity to be heard.

To make exit interviews productive, you must ask yourself what you will do with the information you learn. Here are the answers:

▶ Provide insights about what you need to change within the organization.

▶ Help you discover negative trends or patterns that seem to cause people to perform poorly or to leave.

▶ Help you address training and management issues. Then look to senior management to be the agents of change and to provide the leadership necessary to support these changes.

▶ Help you learn from mistakes, both real and imagined.

14. Prepare for the Employee's First Day of Work

I have conducted numerous exit interviews where the employees mention their first day of work as their first negative experience with the organization. They want to tell me what their first day/week/month was like. Unfortunately, this is not surprising because people never forget their first impressions. It is burned in employees' minds forever, especially if it was a bad experience. You do not want to dash the hopes of a new employee by saying "I'm sorry. Is today your first day? I thought you were starting *next* Monday." Or worse, "I'm sorry, I'm embarrassed. I don't know who you are." Your lack of preparation tells the candidate how much you value him.

You must make sure that your organization always makes a good first impression for every new employee. For starters, be prepared for a new employee's arrival. Your commitment to the employee should be the same as the commitment you expect from him or her. Develop a system that addresses the needs of the new employee. Have the desk ready, the phone hooked up, the chair in place, a few pencils out, a company mug on the desk, and the computer humming. Is this possible all the time? Perhaps not. But if your are unprepared in any way, apologize, tell the candidate when you will rectify the situation, put reasonable accommodations in place, and see that the candidate is happy and comfortable.

15. Communicate Opportunities

Employees of corporate America have a disturbing perception about job advancement: If you want a promotion and a raise, find a job with another company. It is much easier than trying to get ahead in your current company. This type of thinking is deadly to an organization for two reasons:

It kills retention. What message could possibly be worse for an organization than to have its own people believe that if they want to get ahead they have to leave? And usually, your employees will leave—for better opportunities and more money—after they have formed solid relationships (with co-workers and clients) and become truly productive.

It is true! Most companies deny that this is a part of their culture, especially at the senior levels of management. Quite frankly, senior management is often so out of touch with what their employees think. I had a CEO once tell me that there were absolutely no company politics in his organization. How do you even respond to such an inane comment? The reality is, for most every company, you must leave in order to advance. Even if this were not true, perception equals reality, and most employees perceive this to be true. If I had a dollar for every employee who told me he or she was leaving for career advancement, I wouldn't need to be writing this book. You must help end this perception (and reality) within your organization.

Most companies look to the outside for new employees at the senior level because they simply can't see promoting from the inside. Here are two reasons:

- ▶ Employees are judged more for their foibles than their successes because people who know you expect more out of you. Consequently, the people you know and associate with have difficulty advancing. This happens to all of us as we become known entities and the warts and wrinkles that we hid so well in the interviewing process begin to come to the surface.

- ▶ The allure of a new candidate is strong. Unknown candidates provide more hope and promise than known employees because we don't know of their past failures. One thing is for sure. The perfection we hope for in a new candidate is simply unrealistic. My advice is to look hard within your organization before you bring in someone from the outside.

POLICY OR POLITICS?

Most companies, especially larger, more "sophisticated" ones have processes that let employees know there is an opening in another part of the organization. And, of course, everyone is "encouraged to apply." This is the official line, but politics very often get in the way of making this policy a reality. The policy is much more the ideal than the truth. Employees can be afraid to apply because of political issues between groups, and the applicants very often get caught in the middle of the firestorm. Employees may wonder, "What happens if they find out I applied? Will it hurt my career? What if I do not get the position? Will they tell me I am no longer needed in my current position?" I do understand managers wanting to hold on to their best people. But it is far worse to lose your best employees to the competition.

To alleviate fears and to promote a healthy company culture, do the following:

▶ Develop an efficient, effective system to announce new positions. Use the email or intranet.

▶ Keep the system up to date. Post the positions as soon as they are approved.

▶ Make a commitment with your managers not to "guilt trip" or pressure employees to stay in their current positions. You should not take personally an employee's desire to advance and better herself.

▶ Respond quickly to employees who apply.

▶ Feel free to compare outside candidates with internal candidates.

▶ Always hire the best candidate for the position. Evaluate all candidates equally.

▶ Do not feel pressured to hire a candidate because it is the "right thing to do."

CREATE "STRETCH" POSITIONS

Advertising agencies seem to employ the most creative minds, especially those representing technology firms. If only corporate types could have 1 percent of the creativity when it comes to employment situations. What prevents them from creating original, inspired employment solutions? What should you do with an employee who is one of a kind—creative, driven, multitalented, and has no place left to go? First, you should *not* let this person walk out the door to another company. You must be creative and find something that will suit the candidate's need for growth and development, at the same time meeting the company's need for the candidate's talent. Create a "stretch" position. For example, suppose you do not need your very talented CIO for six months. Perhaps you can use her as an internal consultant that works as a troubleshooter with different departments. What about a position as a liaison between engineering and marketing that travels and talks to customers about what is good about your company's products and services? Before you consider letting your valued employees go, make sure you have done all you can to keep them.

16. Identify Your Best Talent

Surely you guard your pearls and diamonds more than your rhinestones. Do the same with your employees. Identify your superstars and work to keep them. One of the objectives of management should be to identify the superstars and build a cocoon around them to make it all the more difficult for them to leave. The first step is to define your employees:

Superstars Simply the best. They can play many positions and can always be counted on to perform on a consistent basis to deliver excellence.

Potential superstars The next wave of superstars. They are merely light on experience or mentoring. They have potential and are the future of your company.

Average players The majority of employees in most organizations. They are good enough to be productive and valued, but are missing the breadth, drive, and super talent needed to be a superstar. There is nothing wrong with being average. Most of us are.

Below average players People who are better off working for the competition. They do poor work with no motivation. Most companies do not weed them out, but they should. Replace them, at the very least, with new average players.

If you and your company are taking retention seriously, you must identify the superstars and potential superstars, and follow these rules:

Pay them what they are worth! These employees should be paid at or above market value at all times. It is your responsibility to know what the market is paying. Never allow your superstars to think they could be making more money elsewhere. If you find that salaries need to be adjusted upward to meet market conditions, do so. Do not wait for your people to come to you first. Keep in mind that compensation is not just base salary. Look at benefits, stock options, bonuses, merit increases, and anything else to help your employees feel you are looking out for them. Lee Silver, president of L.A. Silver, Inc., an international search and consulting firm located in Framingham, Massachusetts, refers to this as "the care and feeding of your organization."

Conduct employee reviews regularly. Employee reviews used to be done once or twice a year. This is not an effective way of providing feedback to employees regarding their progress. Effective performance management requires continual, open dialogue with your employees. Check in with them on a weekly or monthly basis. Document your conversations. You want to avoid a situation where, at the six-month review, your employee thinks he is doing really well and you think otherwise.

17. Make Sure Your Managers Can and Want to Manage

How often does this happen? Your employees do well in their positions and are promoted to managers. Then, the beginning of disaster. People are not necessarily good managers just because they are good employees. Some don't even want the role or responsibility. But, as companies grow, you need more good managers, so your best contributors are given the golden opportunity to manage. With a raise and reassurances, they are sent on their way with no training and no real understanding that their new role will be significantly different from their old job. Poor management, either from lack of ability or lack of training, leads to all sorts of serious problems. To avoid disaster and to help retain your best employees, do not automatically promote your best players to management positions. Take the time to evaluate all needs.

Your organization should have more than one track for advancement. There should be a track that advances employees in the traditional route to management. However, for employees who wish to remain in their original roles or are not candidates for management, there should be a separate track that allows for career advancement. Forcing a good employee to manage or forcing one to remain in a role that offers no opportunities will hurt retention. Both types of employees will end up leaving your organization in search of better opportunities.

MANAGEMENT TIPS

Every company should require basic management training, to teach the basics of good management to new managers. (New managers include those who have managed before but are newly hired within your company.) There is more than one way to manage, so the training your organization offers should teach content and principles, and concern itself less with style. Here are the basics for new managers:

► Communicate with your team on a regular basis. Be sure you meet as a team at least once a week. Keep the meetings short and focused. If you can, hold a meeting on Monday to discuss issues of the upcoming week and one on Friday to review your progress and to plan for the following week.

► Know your employees' strengths and weaknesses. You will be more effective at assigning projects, cross training, and coaching team members on becoming more well-rounded employees.

► Keep the speeches to a minimum. People tend to react, respond, and learn better when you converse with them one on one.

► Praise in public, criticize in private. There are no exceptions to this rule. It is astounding the number of managers who criticize employees in front of their team.

► Make sure all of your team members have goals and understand how important their contributions are to the organization. Make clear how their work supports the company's overall mission.

► Do not punish failure. You will end up creating a culture that does not allow people to take risks. Life begins outside of your comfort zone. Your employees' growth and development require the same.

► Leave your ego at home. Big egos sink business deals and careers. Confidence is fine, but big egos are not.

► The best managers are more like coaches than managers. They praise people for their strengths and patiently work with them on their weaknesses. They jump in only when needed.

► As an employee, it is your job to keep your boss' boss off your boss' back. As a manager, it is your job to keep your boss off your team's back. Allowing your supervisor to manage your team will create confusion.

► Keep morale up. No company is perfect. Allow people to vent but keep them focused on the positive while doing what you can to alleviate the pain they feel.

When an Employee Decides to Leave

What should you do if an employee decides to leave? Mobilize the troops and see what can be done to persuade him or her to stay? Make a counteroffer? Perhaps. But consider this: If an employee gives notice once and then stays because of a counteroffer, it makes it easier for him to repeat the threat. I once consulted with a company that made four counteroffers to an employee within a three-year period. Obviously this employee really wanted to leave. I advised my client not to make any more counteroffers. The employee left within six months.

You must look at each case individually. Sometimes counteroffers are necessary and effective; sometimes you simply have to let go. Regardless, it is vital that you see an employee's resignation in a new light. Don't look at it as your employee quitting, but rather, that he or she is moving on. We must be able to accommodate the needs of some candidates who simply need to move on. I had a conversation with a vice president of human resources last week—a very well-respected person and someone I admire. But his attitude was shortsighted regarding one of his key software managers leaving and taking a new job. This manager was taken to lunch by his co-workers, and the vice president refused to participate. He said, "My job is to keep them here, not to buy them nachos when they leave. I consider him leaving a personal failure."

If you make a villain out of an employee because he or she decides to leave, that person will feel it. You will end up missing out on all the potential opportunities this employee could bring to you and your organization in the future. Instead, if a great employee is leaving, acknowledge it. Understand that even after the employee leaves, the relationship lives on. He or she could be

- ▶ A valued customer

- ▶ A new employee (again)

- ▶ A strategic business partner

- ▶ A vendor

- ▶ A key component of a strategic relationship

In simple terms, this former employee can add as much or more value to your organization than if he or she were still your employee— by being a champion for your company—a valued contact who can support your successes as you support his. Here are ways you can maintain the valuable relationships with your former employees:

▶ Invite them to your holiday parties.

▶ Keep them on your mailing list.

▶ Invite them to corporate functions.

▶ Keep in touch and find out how the new job is going.

▶ Help them in any way you can.

Retention, like hiring, is not an exact science. But if you create an organization, a culture, and an infrastructure that address the issues and support the hiring and retention process, you will begin to win more than you lose. You will build a solid foundation that will support a strong company.

7

Notes from the Underground

Just as the Olympic marathoner takes a victory lap after running more than 26 miles, I need to take that extra lap in the form of one more chapter. In some ways, this was the toughest chapter to write because it's my last opportunity to make sure I've covered all the bases. So, here goes. To the company leaders out there: The first section of "Notes from the Underground" is written especially for you. The last section is specifically for managers, employees, and prospective candidates searching for that better opportunity.

For the Leaders

Making the Right Hire Is Job One

You build a great business by making the right hiring choices. Period. That's why my primary focus in this book is on the hiring process and doing it right. That process must also be supported by your efforts to retain your employees. Hire the best people, support their efforts, tend to their needs, don't micromanage, and work to retain them for as long as possible. Growing companies are fueled by great people and great people build strong companies.

Commit to Setting the Only Acceptable Standards

If you are charged with leading and running a company, you owe it to your employees and customers to lead by example. Here are a few tips on how to get started.

- ► Hire consultants to help you to evaluate and make recommendations that will address your organization's problems. There are great consultants in virtually every discipline. Use their expertise to support and guide your efforts to meet your corporate objectives. Be sure all consultants are checked out and rechecked for their ability to deliver, and always be sure that consultants have a clear understanding of the problem, the budget, and the deliverables.

- ► Develop a mission statement that speaks to what your company is trying to accomplish—its values and operating principles.

- ► Conduct an employee and customer survey. According to Bruce Katcher, an organizational psychologist who specializes in employee and customer surveys and president of the Discovery Group (www.discoverysurveys.com), "employee surveys help management gain a clear understanding of how employees feel about their work lives, what's most important to them, and how their commitment to the organization can be improved. On the other hand, customer satisfaction surveys help organizations assess how well they are meeting the expectations of the customers; identify desired improvements in their products and services; and learn what is really important to their customers."

Both will help in retaining two of your organization's most valuable assets:

- ► Its employees

- ► Its customers

- ► Identify the best practices within your industry, then work to achieve them within your organization. If you want to be one of the best, you have to do either what the best are doing or take a giant step and improve on what the best are doing.

- ► Establish a career development program that will allow people to see clear paths for professional growth and development. Many good companies have technical career paths and many have managerial career paths. Great companies have both. Couple this with solid training programs, tuition reimbursement, and mentoring programs and you give employees another reason to stay with your organization, as opposed to going to another, when they want to advance their career.

- ► Keep apprised of what the competition is doing within your industry. If you do this, you will be more aware of what is happening within your own world and be able to make more informed decisions based on new trends, ideas, and observations. You do not have to copy every new age fad and idea of the week, but you should be able to sort the sane from the nonsense and use what is viable to tweak your own organization's effectiveness.

- ► Stay informed about what companies are doing in *other* industries. Great ideas often come not from the myopic viewpoints of your own industry but from other industries. Learn who sets the new standards for customer service, speed of delivery, and ability to cut costs. Perhaps you can apply it to your business. You may not be in the delivery business but I bet you can learn a bit from FedEx's customer service, as they are clearly one of the standard setters. Is your customer service that good? Why not?

- ► Judiciously upgrade your workforce where and when necessary.

- ► Develop a CPO (Chief People Officer) position within your company. The right person in this position will be responsible for the "care and feeding" of your employees. (See Chapter 6.)

- ► Introduce and establish new and creative reward systems.

These ideas are to help you, the leader, take action and make your organization better—a more efficient, effective, enjoyable place to work. Doing nothing should be unacceptable to you. You owe it to yourself and your organization to live up to the leadership potential you have. Success breeds success. Another step, another accomplishment. Join the ranks of organizations that understand perfection is not just a place but a direction. Keep in mind, you will not turn the company around in a day, week, or quarter. However, you will be amazed at the progress you can make, day after day with deliberate, goal-oriented effort. The world is full of examples of people who took over C-grade companies that had languished for years and turned them into winners. Life is too short to work for a bad company and even worse, to own and run one. I have seen so many people make the commitment to turn companies around and succeed. You can do the same. As a leader, you are responsible for your employees' careers, quality of life in the workplace, mortgages, car payments, and children's college tuitions. Commit to improve all you do and set the only acceptable standard as one of excellence. Lead by example, remain focused, be consistent, reward excellence, assume intelligent risks, and see just how far this commitment can take you and your organization.

Communicate Often, Effectively, and Purposefully

Tom Kennedy, president of The Kennedy Group (www.kennedy-groupboston.com), has been assisting companies, both large and small, for over ten years. He teaches strategic corporate communication, including how to do effective presentations and public speaking. Tom always tells people that the ultimate success of what you say depends entirely on how well you say it. Tom's ultimate message? The CEO is the communications leader and sets the standard for the company to follow. How a company communicates with its people is absolutely critical. As a corporate leader, you must consider how you communicate with the following people:

- ▶ Customers

- ▶ Investors

- ▶ Partners

- ▶ Vendors

- ▶ Employees

▶ Board members

▶ The media

How you communicate can determine not only the direction, but also the very life of the organization you lead.

Former Vermont governor, Madeleine Kunin, is a popular speaker at business schools across the country. She says that the ability to communicate effectively is the number-one quality of effective leadership, and those who do not speak well cannot lead. She adds that few are born with this skill, and the rest are taught.

Virtually all successful CEOs are excellent communicators, but their presentation and public-speaking skills are poor. Reading aloud the text on PowerPoint or printing out slides as handouts has become the method of choice for making presentations. It puts your audience to sleep. In "Software Sends Words to the Brain, but Can They Stir the Heart?" (*The New York Times,* April 17, 1999), Laurence Zuckerman says that PowerPoint (and other similar software) "debases" presentations, and has "taken the life out of public speaking by homogenizing it at a low level," producing presentations that are "devoid of original ideas." In "Death by PowerPoint" (*Small Business Computing,* April 18, 2001), Angela Garber says, "Tools like presentation programs can quickly become crutches, and even get in the way of effective communication." Great speakers like Ronald Reagan, Bill Clinton, Lou Gerstner, and Jack Welch know that *they* are the visual. They rarely use slides, if at all, and when they do, only if the slides are truly a visual *aid*.

The pain caused by poor communications skills is abundant. I quote from two recent Kiplinger newsletters: "Almost half of all CEOs write their annual meeting presentations on the plane en route! No wonder we fall asleep!" and "Most salespeople don't have a prepared presentation. The top 20 percent have prepared, rehearsed, and finely tuned presentations."

Leading business schools in the United States are just beginning to recognize the need for presentation training and incorporating it into their core curriculum. Many MBAs have found that, although they possess solid business skills, their communication skills are lacking. Communication is much more than PR. It involves tools that require you to present a mission and a message (or product) and do it clearly and effectively. Furthermore, intellectual knowledge is just a small part of communicating effectively. You must connect with people emotionally. Jack Welch,

CEO of General Electric, says "Businesses are powered by emotions and feelings as much as by money, knowledge, logic, and technology."

General Electric is noted for providing excellent communications skills training to its employees, especially to its senior managers. Lou Gerstner, CEO of IBM, recently required all senior executives to participate in presentation and public-speaking training and coaching. This is no small investment in time, effort, and resources. However, the best communicators recognize the value of this investment. The ability to convey an effective, focused, concise, and memorable message is a great achievement and one worth developing.

Make HR Part of the Management Team

Stating the obvious, the most successful companies get a quality product or service to market in the least amount of time. Corporate leaders pray for the workforce that can achieve these results for its company. These organizations provide a workplace that answers the all-important question all employees have: "What's in it for me?"

Employees no longer simply look for flex time or compensation packages that fit their needs. Today's workforce require the following:

- ▶ To be led, not managed

- ▶ The opportunity for intellectual and technical growth (in the form of skills development programs)

- ▶ To have a workplace where they are respected and recognized for their particular skills, talents, and potential; where employee retention is a priority

- ▶ To have the opportunity to be creative and appreciated for that creativity

- ▶ To have an environment where learning from mistakes is the norm, not just a cliché (not a culture that punishes failure or criticizes people for taking chances)

- ▶ An organization that believes mistakes are for learning and are analyzed by real processes

- ▶ To use the analyses for evolving the next generation of a product, service, or project

All of this means that top executives must be highly effective in technical, business, and relational skills, leading employees to be dedicated and highly skilled themselves. This can be much more crucial than having finely honed financial, sales, marketing, or other functional process skills. It is essential that you move from managing to leading, often requiring a far greater change in relational skills and expertise than many of today's management people truly understand. Leading requires you to

► Formulate, articulate, and make the reality (or business objective) understandable.

► Thank participants for their contributions to the success.

► (Most importantly) be a servant—removing barriers to create processes that enable every individual to do his or her best to contribute new ideas, products, and process improvements creatively—to take the best service or product to market in the least amount of time. This requires great leadership, not management.

The successful environment today is truly one of team functioning. Much like a baseball team, achievement requires a coach and an organization that trains and develops team members to their highest level of capability, as defined by the players themselves, and is aligned with the organization's objectives. Each player wants to be highly respected for his or her work and contributions; each player has to be accountable for doing a job well.

All that said, the human resources department must develop their business skills much in the same manner as the executive team and finance, sales, manufacturing, and operations departments must develop their relational skills. Top executive teams poised for success include top HR executives as core members of their team. Including HR in the executive team shows the employees that the workforce is being included in the development and success of an organization. It takes the equal participation of each functional area to produce results. The people, business processes, and technical components unite to enable the achievement of individual and company objectives.

The human resources function that exists today is a far cry from the administrative duties that were performed in the early days when HR was called the "Personnel" department. Due to all the changing requirements of a growing, complex business environment, a strong HR influence is vital and necessary. If you are a member of the human resources team in your organization, you should continually increase your knowledge of general business trends, requirements, and processes, and familiarize yourself with and become an expert on the company's use and application of technology. You should strive to be more creative at understanding and analyzing individual and company objectives, and integrating the human factors into ongoing business processes. Ensure that all HR contributions are potential enablers of achievement for the individual and company. Your company's employee retention will rely on the ability of the entire leadership team, including HR, to develop an environment that answers the "What's in it for me?" question.

It is in the best interest of corporate leadership to make a place for HR at the highest levels of senior management, and include HR in the planning processes within the organization. This isn't to justify HR's existence. I have seen so many problems occur within organizations that were avoidable. The HR professionals of today could have saved many companies a lot of time, money, and grief had they been involved in all processes from the start rather than having been brought in during or after a crisis. With recruiting, retention, and corporate culture at the top of the list of importance in a strong, effective organization, every company needs HR as a partner on the management team.

How to Get the Best Out of HR

First, hire the very best HR people into your organization. To be successful, you must seek the characteristics that are highly desirable. The three listed below are the core competencies you should look for, but finding candidates with all three will be very tough. You will have to make compromises and decide for yourself which characteristics to weigh more heavily than the others. HR managers should

- ► Be business-oriented thinkers who understand all aspects of your business

- ► Have technical knowledge, use it, and apply it according to the organization's requirements

- ► Be relational (relationship oriented), have the ability to earn the respect and consideration of those with whom they consult, and be able to influence processes when necessary

The leader and executive team must work with HR in the early stages of processes to develop plans relating to culture, performance management, organizational development, corporate goals, operating principles, and reward systems.

Pay Vendors on Time

I have dealt with CFOs who feel vendors are a dime a dozen. Regardless of whether you believe this, however, *good* vendors are priceless. They are the ones who deliver emergency supplies to you on a Saturday. They tell you about special pricing or feed you valuable market information. They add value to your organization that is clearly above and beyond the call of duty in an attempt to build a relationship. Do not "reward" them by paying their invoices late. I understand the need for companies to institute payment delay policies in a down economy. If you must be late, call the vendor and tell him or her when to expect payment. There are so many companies that don't. Promote good will. Be a standout, impress your vendors, and pay on time (or early), if possible. Watch and see what type of service this will get you.

Earn Respect

The surest road to not getting respect is to demand it. Respect must, in all cases, be earned. Treat people fairly, act with integrity, lead with grace and dignity, and communicate openly and honestly. If you can do this, you are well on your way to the respect you so abundantly deserve.

When Seeking Venture Capital, Use an Outside Firm to Help

I have seen very bright people with very good ideas spend inordinate amounts of time searching for venture capital and have nothing to show for it. Raising capital for a new company can be a long, hard struggle if not handled correctly from the start. It takes experts and is best left to the pros who do it for a living. They know all the ins and outs of what needs to be addressed and can answer the VC's questions even before they are asked. Charles Collier, co-founder of Mount Vernon Strategies (a strategic management and consulting firm in Boston, www.mvstrat.com), told me once about a phone call he received from a client. This client needed to raise $50 million "and needed a business plan yesterday!" Having an outside consultant create the business plan allowed the client to present a business strategy to venture capital firms that addressed most of the potential concerns the VCs might have had. The client was able to present themselves in a more organized, strategic manner than if they had attempted to act on their own. One other thing to consider: When raising money, be sure to raise enough. If not, you will find yourself continually looking for more money to fund the company instead of dedicating your time to building and running the organization.

When Interviewing, Make a Good First Impression

The hiring process is similar to the justice system: They are both flawed, but they are all we've got. The parts that work, work well. But, the justice system sometimes allows innocent people to sit in jail and the guilty to go free. In the hiring process, the wrong people can get the job and the right ones could be sent packing. In both cases, only later do we learn of our mistakes (if we learn them at all), and then we simply put the blame on the system. However, many times it isn't the system that fails. A few weeks ago I had breakfast with a friend who is a highly respected executive. She told me the sad story of her husband, an exceedingly prominent executive, who had an interview with a well-known company. The interviewer was an executive vice president. He showed up almost 30 minutes late, made no apologies, put his feet up on the desk, and opened the interview with the following question: "So, what do you want to be when you grow up?" The interviewer was in his late 30s, and he was interviewing someone in his early 50s. Then the interviewer proceeded to unwrap a sandwich and eat it during the interview. The interviewer's behavior was reprehensible and unprofessional. When you interview, always be on your best behavior; you are representing your organization. Consider the following:

- ▶ Always be on time. If you are more than five minutes late, apologize. If you are going to be more than fifteen minutes late, contact the candidate, if possible, or arrange for someone to meet your candidate when he or she arrives for the interview, explaining that your are running late and when you can be expected.

- ▶ If you are going to be delayed, see that the candidate gets refreshments: water, coffee, tea, soda. Some candidates are nervous and will not ask. Your unexpected delay can make for a very long and tense interview, so making sure the candidate is comfortable ahead of time can alleviate the problem.

- ▶ Be prepared. Read the candidate's résumé. Don't fake it. If you did not read it, apologize, and read it on the spot. If you say you read it and didn't, the candidate will know. Familiarize yourself with the position for which you are interviewing.

▶ Be pleasant, courteous, and gracious. Make sure the candidate leaves with nothing other than a positive image of you and the organization you represent.

This is not designed to be a lesson in manners. However, I have seen enough examples of embarrassing or poor behavior among interviewers that I felt it necessary to include this information to help people represent their organizations well.

Have a Real Person Answer Phones

I have learned to live with voice-activated systems that greet you when you call a company. And although I know it is not feasible to expect a real person to answer every call, it doesn't mean I have to like it. In a world where everyone has gotten so accustomed to hearing an automated system, it is refreshing to have a real person as your first point of contact. If at all possible, find money in the budget to hire a person to answer phones. Be creative, if necessary, and hire someone on an internship basis or develop a job share program among two or three administrators. Your customers will appreciate being recognized by name when they call.

Require Candidates to Sign a Non-Disclosure Agreement

A non-disclosure agreement (NDA) is a legal document stating that the person who signs will not discuss your business with anyone from outside your organization. An NDA must be drawn up by a contract attorney. Do not try to develop one yourself or use someone else's. All vendors, employees, and candidates should sign them. Confidentiality and speed to market are critical to your company's success. So, whenever it is necessary for someone to know the details of your business, have him or her sign an NDA. If a person refuses to sign, refuse to deal with him. Confidentiality is critical, especially in the early stages of building and running a business. I know from attending numerous networking events that people talk openly about everything. Protect your investment with an NDA.

Use Email Judiciously

Using email limits your ability to really communicate effectively, especially on important issues. I love using email and probably use it more than most people. But I know the proper time and place for its use. Email is invaluable when needing just a few words of explanation on a subject, to introduce the purpose of sending an attachment, to change meeting times, to comment on a report or idea, or to request a meeting. You should use email to convey bits of information to a group of people on a mailing list. Do not use email to facilitate discussions among a group of people or to conduct an important, difficult, or involved conversation. People tend to communicate by email because they would rather not deal with each other on a more personal level. An appropriate communication method is vital to the proper day-to-day functions of an organization. It is absolutely impossible to conduct meaningful business-oriented, strategic, philosophical, planning-related discussion via email. You will also miss the subtleties—the passion, vocal inflections, facial expressions, and body language that make communication effective and significant.

▸ Email is ideal for quick, simple communication related to business that can be transacted in an easy manner.

▸ Phone calls are for communication that requires more thoughtful and creative conversation.

▸ Real face-to-face meetings are best when the parties involved consider the objectives of their conversation to be of a critical nature, requiring more complete and open communication.

For Managers, Employees, and Prospective Candidates

Running a business is easy if you don't know how; difficult if you do. That is about as true a statement as you will ever hear. If you have no idea how to run a business, it's a cakewalk. My wife (the smart one of the team) and I were once hired to advise the CEO of an organization, but he did not listen or follow our advice. (Ironically, he had brought us on board for the very purpose of advising him.) He thought he knew better and did as he pleased, with bad results. The lesson here is if you need help in running an organization and then you ask for assistance, listen to the people you have chosen to support your efforts. There are times when your instincts may be correct and your advisors are wrong. In these cases, fire your advisors and choose ones you are comfortable with.

Do Not Submit a Résumé If You Are Not Qualified for the Position

Recruiters (agency, corporate, and HR) are inundated by résumés from people who are not qualified for the position for which they are

applying. I am not saying the applicants are a *bit* off the mark. I am saying they are not even *close* to having the skills, background, or experience necessary to do the job. These people play the "hit or miss" game,
thinking there might be a match somewhere in the company for their
talents. This is not the way it works in the real world. Recruiters often
receive well over 150 résumés for a given position. I once advertised for
a vice president of marketing position in Philadelphia and received
almost 900 responses. It was a nightmare. How on earth do you review
and qualify 900 résumés? It is a tremendous waste of the recruiter's
time and will do very little to endear you to that recruiter. I understand that people send in résumés because they feel they have nothing
to lose, but in reality, they gain very little. As a recruiter, I would rather
have a person call me, out of the blue, and ask for help. I could, perhaps, offer to give him the opportunity to tap into my Rolodex for people to network with. At least this way, I also make a new contact, add
him or her to my network, and can help out in a way that makes some
real sense. So please, if you don't even approach the qualifications,
don't send in your résumé. It makes the recruiter question your judgment and does very little to further your cause.

Allow People to Do Their Jobs

I continue to see situations where employees are given the responsibility to do a job but are not given the authority to make the decisions
to do whatever is necessary to get the job done. Do not assign responsibilities without assigning authority. Otherwise, you will tie people's
hands in a way that turns them into producers of excuses and poor
results rather than producers of great work. In his book *The Simple
Art of Greatness: Building, Managing, and Motivating a Kick-Ass Workforce,* Jim Mullen references Aristotle by saying "For every right, Aristotle taught, there is a corresponding responsibility; and for every
responsibility there is a concordant right."

Simply stated, this powerful dialectic teaches us that when you give
an employee the responsibility of getting something done, you automatically assign that employee with all of the authority necessary to be
successful. But so many employees struggle and fail on a regular basis.
Why? Management does not give their employees the authority to do
whatever is necessary to get the job done. As Mullen says, it is management, not the employee, that bears the responsibility for unsatis-
factory work. Instead of trying to micromanage, the better solution is

to hire smart people and let them do their jobs. Provide them with the authority necessary to produce superior work instead of a compromise that results in work the employee is not proud of and you are not satisfied with. Decentralize authority, let people do their jobs, and watch for the success that comes from an empowered workforce.

Do Not Give References

Institute a corporate policy of never giving references under any circumstances. Make sure it is understood and observed across the board and that the entire organization follows the directive. Do not make exceptions for anyone, including the executive team, CEO, or yourself. CEOs are not in a protected position that shields them from litigation. Here are some basic rules to follow:

▶ Do not go into your office, close the door, and give a reference to someone you "know and trust" because you feel it is safe. The rule was established for a reason—to protect you and your organization.

▶ Do not give out references even if they are "personal" references. It will put you in dangerous territory because it takes you away from limiting your discussions to job performance, duties, and professional responsibilities, and draws you into talking about the person on a more personal level.

Avoid costly mistakes. If a person calls for a reference, refer that person to human resources, who should then provide the following information:

▶ Confirmation of the former employee's dates of employment

▶ Last position title at the organization

End of story. Do not give out any more information than this. People will try to pressure you because they have nothing to lose. Resist the pressure, inform the person of the corporate policy, and end the discussion.

Do Not Hire Candidates Who Make You Uncomfortable

I am a fanatic motorcyclist. Sometimes I find myself on roads that make me very uncomfortable. I have no explanation for it, but I feel my chest tighten as I proceed along the road. What exactly bothered me about that turn? That stretch of road? That intersection? My solution is to avoid the areas of road that make me uncomfortable. I do the same when it comes to candidates. I do not hire them if they make me uncomfortable. Sometimes I interview them several times to see if I can get over the feeling. If I can't, I don't hire. It's not to exercise power. It's based on personal experiences: Candidates I hired who initially made me uncomfortable wound up not living up to my expectations. I don't call it intuition or sixth sense. But after being in so many hiring situations, I figure I must have developed a level of expertise and judgment that enables me to assess a candidate using more than just a résumé. Very often I can figure out my source of discomfort. A candidate makes an unusual remark, behaves in a manner that seems outside the norm, or simply is unable to answer certain questions. If you can pinpoint the source of discomfort, you can analyze the problem and move on. If you are unsure, check in with another member of the interviewing team to help you figure out the source of discomfort. At the end of the day, if you are still left feeling cold, do not make the hire.

Understand the Difference Between Coaching and Management

Coaching is not a fad or a buzzword. It is not here today, gone tomorrow "pop company culture" claptrap. Coaching is here to stay. So is management. The most successful organizations have individuals who can straddle the fence and do both based on the specific needs of the business at the moment.

▶ Coaching is more collaborative and exploratory. It takes good listening skills to be a good coach.

▶ Traditional management tends to be more authoritative and controlling.

▶ Coaches work on team development. They play to the strengths of each member while trying to improve their weaknesses. Coaching is more about employee empowerment, trust, influence, facilitation, development, and delivery of expected results.

▶ Management is more about using your staff to get the job done. It is about planning, leading, organizing, controlling, and delivering the expected results.

There are no real value judgments here. Both require the delivery of the desired result, and excellence is still expected from all players. How do you, as a manager, get your people to perform? Coaching and more traditional management both have their good and bad points. Be aware of the differences and use them to get your best results.

Learn to Laugh in the Workplace

Laughter is an absolute requirement for a healthy workplace. It is the great stress reliever, helping us to get through the stresses of meetings and deadlines. Years ago I met Loretta LaRoche (www.stressed.com), author and lecturer, who talks about the importance of stress management and humor in the workplace. I learned a lot from her. In almost all cases, we take ourselves far too seriously. Learn to laugh in the workplace and start by laughing at yourself.

Politic Wisely

Politics exist in every organization, both large and small. This fact of business is inescapable. With this in mind, it is important to remember that when you politic, you must do it for the good of the company. For example, if you support a co-worker's proposal, don't do it because he supported your proposal last month. Do it because you believe it is in the best interest of the organization. If your motivation is out of dislike, revenge, or because you owe someone a favor, you are not acting for the benefit of the company. Try your best to put agendas aside. You will avoid having to wrestle with your conscience. Plus, you will have the satisfaction of knowing that all your efforts and activities have been for the greater good of the company.

Employee, Train Thyself

Good employees want to become better at what they do. For example, technologists like to keep up with the latest technology so they can make a contribution to the organization and remain marketable should they have to change jobs. Good companies offer training to their employees. Training is a partnership. It takes a meeting of the minds between management and employees to make it happen. Employees, be reasonable in your expectations of company training. If the training you need is not offered, be proactive. If you, as an employee, are reasonable in your expectations, work for the changes you feel are needed, and also try to learn some things on your own. You will find your value to both the organization and yourself will rise if you follow this path.

Life Begins Outside Your Comfort Zone

What an amazing year for me. I lost 36 pounds, joined Toastmasters, started lecturing, and was elected vice president of membership of my Toastmasters club. I even wrote a book! (The experience was a mixture of exhaustion, exhilaration, frustration, long nights, and ultimately, very satisfying.) Beginning in January 2001, each and every day was lived way out of my comfort zone. But I did have advisors and experts to call upon when the need for help became apparent. Now it's July, and I am a true believer that life begins outside of your comfort zone. Strangely enough, I seem to have become comfortable with the discomfort. Prior to this year I was mostly too comfortable with my own existence. I have learned a great deal about what can be done by stretching and doing what you have never done before. And look at what I've been able to accomplish! Life and its rewards are much more satisfying when the stakes are high. I am thinking about skydiving in September with some friends. Here's hoping the chute opens.

A

An Interview with a World-Class Recruiter

Interviewee: Martin Levin, recruiting operations manager for the U.S., Gentronics.

M r. Levin has a wealth of knowledge and more than 25 years of recruiting experience in technology companies of all sizes. His overview of the IT industry has great depth, and he can speak to recruiting from years of experience and perspective. This interview was conducted and designed to complement and reinforce the chapters in this book.

HA: Let's say you have a situation where you are told your client requires 35 or 40 people for a call center, or perhaps 50 people in the IT department. There are certain things you have to do first, at the planning stage, so things go smoothly. What do you do to get the recruiting and hiring process going?

ML: We initiate the process by determining the number of people necessary and in which areas of the country we will focus. We recruit people all over the U.S., so we have to find out where the locations are going to be. From there we put a strategy plan together—the best way to start sourcing these people. The positions are identified, and then we sit down with the hiring managers to understand the criteria to hire the right person. We carefully scrutinize the open requisition to make sure we understand all the requirements—what the [fine points] are according to the manager—for hiring the right person. What does the right person have to have in order to get hired? What constitutes a good hiring decision? Once that has been discussed and agreed upon, and once we've decided on recruiting locations, here at Gentronics, we go into our résumé database and do a search by location and skill set to find people who are available. Then we identify the prospects and send inquiries, through the database and email, asking them whether they are available or are interested in the positions. Next, we consider posting the positions on a variety of Internet boards, to see what kind of responses we get. Some are posted on niche boards, depending on the type of positions, and some are posted on general boards. We track to see what response we are getting from the postings. Also, we direct an email blitz on our internal people for employee referrals, making them aware of the position and to encourage our workforce to help with recruiting by offering a reward for referrals. Once this starts the flow of prospects, we begin screening people. Also, in some situations, the hiring manager knows where some of these referrals might work. If that is the case, we do a "back door" search through a researcher we have available who confirms the identity of these companies. Then we try to approach others within the companies to make contact with these people. It is an indirect way to recruit and make contact, using a third party. It might network us to someone else who is currently looking for a position. We would accept their résumés, too. If we find we are not getting a certain quantity or quality of people, we consider other sources to bring people in. Certainly, if there is going to be a job fair in the vicinity where we need people, we would consider going to the job fair or posting the positions at the job fair's general site. This could be an avenue for finding people. Another channel is advertising in the local papers, not for big money, but in a given community, to see what we uncover. Many of the local papers have a connecting website where you can list the positions.

HA: You mentioned the employee referral program. I have always thought these programs are important, and making them visible leads to something valuable. But if people don't know they exist, it is very difficult for individuals to take part in them. What are your thoughts on the importance of employee referral programs? What do you think of the people you get from these programs? Are they necessarily better than other ways of recruiting? Are people more carefully screened?

ML: An employee referral program is a key avenue in sourcing employees to your company base. We generate knowledge by sending emails on a monthly basis to our workforce, telling them about the hot jobs of the month, reminding them what jobs are available for referrals. When we hire someone, part of the orientation process is to inform them about the employee referrals. We encourage any employee to refer another person, a friend, an acquaintance, or someone in the same working niche. We offer monetary rewards for referrals. Usually, we find that the referrals are usually good employees. The referring employee, in most cases, does not refer a dud, but someone who is capable and has the skills we are looking for. In addition to the emails, we also send out flyers and put up tent cards (i.e., those little folding cards that are sometimes seen in restaurants that list desserts and appetizers) in the cafeteria—throughout the building we have boards with messages that remind employees of the referral programs. During the course of the year, depending on the month, we might spice it up, say, for the holidays. We give gifts or money for referrals. During the summer we make the program more enticing by giving extra money to be used toward vacation. We are constantly putting this information in front of the existing workforce to remind them to assist us to find key qualified people.

HA: It sounds as though the employee referral program tends to work better when there is a new, interesting, or exciting incentive. It seems as though the program is kept in the forefront of people's minds by spicing things up.

ML: Yes, you have to remember the majority of the people you hire, at least for the first year they are with the company, usually have a positive attitude. As I said earlier, it is an extra way for them to earn additional money, and in an indirect way, build the company with talent, and help the company to grow by filling positions as quickly as possible. Certainly in today's market you must do that. You cannot hold a prospective applicant for an extended period of time, otherwise you are going to lose him or her.

HA: Let me ask you this. Sometimes candidates become very difficult to find. At what point do you go to agencies, or do you go to agencies at all?

ML: Certainly, agencies are useful. I do not go to agencies nor will I tell my recruiters to go to agencies at the very beginning. After all methods are exhausted, then we consider going to an agency. As I said, we have a researcher doing a "back door" research to find people, find names, find contact information, and then we call them to see if they are interested, or network to get them. If all fails, we would then consider using an agency, but only an agency with whom we have an agreement prior to making contact. I do not call just any agency out of the blue. We make sure the agency is a reputable agency, with good references, that is not going to try to gouge for fees. I try to keep the fee within 20 percent to 25 percent on the noncontingency type of searches.

HA: What kind of a guarantee do you look for from agencies?

ML: You try to get the best you can, a 90-day guarantee, for a 100 percent reimbursement if the prospective person leaves within that time. You work it out with each agency.

HA: Regarding candidate generation, there is always something new on the Internet. What role do you think the Internet will play during the next year? What is the role of the Internet in sourcing and recruiting candidates as far into the future as you can see, based on what you know?

ML: The Internet is going to become a major tool in recruiting people as was classified advertising many years ago. It is evolving; it can be used to find people in a many ways, on a variety of different sites (niche sites), that represent a given discipline, HR discipline, an IP discipline, a Marketing discipline, a Sales discipline. Also, with the proper software, the Internet could be used to "mine" people ("back-dooring," getting the passive candidate). There are various software packages on the market that will help you mine people—find people through a website or maybe an association roster to which they belong. It may be possible to get into a company's firm list using the software on the Internet to find contact information. At present there is some software we are using. Anytime someone is quoted in the press, it provides us with information. The bio is given, and the software pulls it off the press. The software sets the information up in such a way that we can search by company, last name, degree and/or college. We can go in and find an alumnus from, let's say Harvard, who graduated, perhaps, three years ago. A lot of the information from the software will be contact information, the name, email address, possibly the present employer, past employer, title. This actually helps us get in, do research, and make calls to these people to see if they are interested and maybe do some networking. It is a way to find people who do not actively have their résumés on many sites.

HA: Is this software preshrunk, or is it something you download off the Internet? And are you at liberty to name the software?

ML: You buy the software package. You do not have to install anything. They give you a password; you are using their portal. You buy a seat and the seat entitles you to go into the software, use the password and the code word for your criteria, whether it is a person's name, person's company, school, year, and degree. It then searches various sites on the Internet for anyone who was quoted by the press, and amasses that information. If there are several people in a company who made some comments cited in the press in the past year, the software will sort those people in a hierarchy from the chairman of the board to a lead technician. This is just one tool. There is another particular piece of software called Résumé Robot. We enter the criteria, it searches and pulls people back to us. Doing these things on the Internet is time consuming; you have to look through all of the material you receive. The material is not minutely defined, so it can be vague or ambiguous, which necessitates time and effort to examine it. That is why I split it up [between] a researcher and a recruiter. That seems to be the thing of the future, to have a dedicated researcher who fills the pipeline, takes that pipeline, and passes it on to the recruiter. This frees the recruiter to reference and evaluate the existing candidates.

HA: What was the name of the software you first mentioned?

ML: It is Eliyon Technologies. Hopefully this software will take off, but they exclusively sell it to executive search firms, and they use it in their back rooms to search people. So if they can use it, I can use it also.

HA: Tell me a little bit about interviewing. There have been countless books written on interviewing. I also included an interview section in this book. Everyone is obviously at their very best at that time, and companies are selling their organizations while trying to get employees. What do you think is effective and can you clarify it for those people who don't really understand interviewing; maybe show them how it should be done (as someone who has been doing it for so long)?

ML: Interviewing, to me, is the key factor. The recruiting department is going to open the door to anyone coming in. In a sense that is the first step into an organization. Unfortunately, interviewing is probably the weakest link in any organization. That is probably why you will find organizations going to evaluations or testing or assessments to find and evaluate prospective employees. In my career, I have found a high percentage of hiring managers, who receive candidates from the recruiters, are not trained how to interview properly. They go off on tangents and don't ask proper questions; they do not draw from the applicant what is needed to make the selection, the best selection. I have been trying to install some software that will help the managers to interview properly. Take the job description. From that the software breaks the job description down into proper legal questions. The manager can then pick and choose and evaluate the individual on properties: technical properties; personality properties (introvert or extrovert), and his or her expertise in the skill sets to be used in the job. They can evaluate the applicant's answers, and from that, can determine the benchmark of what makes a good candidate. I find, most of the time, managers hire people they like or that build up rapport rather quickly. Candidates can be coached. There are tricks or techniques you can tell the candidate to do, to gain rapport or respect, to trick the manager who is trying to make a decision. Again, interviewing is extremely important. The majority of people who make the final decisions do not interview properly, do not know how to interview. If you ask whether they have ever been trained to interview, an extremely large number will confess they have never been adequately trained to interview correctly.

HA: That brings me to my next question. At times I have thought of recruiting as part art and part science. I know you have a number of recruiters and have managed large-scale recruiting projects. Have you ever been in a position where you sat down with individuals and taught them how to interview? Have you done any training, and, if so, have you had any success with those trainees?

ML: Yes I have. I have done executive coaching for a number of years, training executives how to interview correctly, how to get past the recruiters, and make a positive impression on hiring managers.

I know I have been successful because people come back and compliment me on my coaching to get them past the recruiting department and get a positive feedback from a hiring manager.

HA: Based on that answer, tell me two or three things a person should never do, and two or three things they should always do when they are interviewing.

ML: Some of the things they should certainly do at an interview are

- ► Be on time for the interview

- ► Be properly dressed for the interview

- ► Be very attentive

- ► Be a good listener; listening is very important at an interview

- ► Being able to "mirror" the interviewer in some of the gestures is important; this creates a rapport with the interviewer

Some small talk is essential. One must be observant when entering an office. Look around to see what pictures or items the interviewer has displayed in the office; they can help break the ice. In the course of interviewing, it is extremely important to go into the interview with some knowledge of the company, what is its scope, what is the product or the service of the company; show you have done your homework prior to the interview. I think, during the course of the interview, it is desirable to make eye contact with the interviewer on a regular basis. Ask questions during the interview and be attentive to what the interviewer is saying.

HA: What about the interviewer? Are there some things the interviewers absolutely must do so they can accurately assess the person being interviewed and make intelligent recommendations to the hiring manager on whether or not the person should move forward?

ML: I think these people should be prepared to properly interview the candidate, spending some time, prior to the interview, to reevaluate the résumé and understand the details of the job description. To review the job description is important to fully understand the type of questions to ask in order to get the results you want, to know on what you are trying to focus and [elicit] from the interviewee. I think you must be a good listener and able to ask challenging questions of the interviewees, to make sure they can think on their feet. These are some important points as well as your inclusion of eye contact. You, the interviewer, have to look interested during the interview.

HA: Moving away from interviewing, sooner or later you have to make a decision on that candidate. How do you go about advising the hiring manager on whether or not to hire the candidate? Furthermore, what thoughts do you have about making a bad hire?

ML: Hiring the wrong person can be a very costly mistake. To clarify, in recruiting, we don't hire. It is the hiring manager who makes the decision. We can give the input to the hiring manager, the person is very open, seems very knowledgeable, would fit into the department you are running, seems to accomplish the task that you need done. Again, we only refer and give comments to the hiring manager. We cannot say, "Yes, you should hire this person" or "No, you should not hire this person." The final decision, no matter what is said, is with the hiring manager. We give our opinions, our views, and hopefully the hiring manager will be receptive and consider the information he has been given. In many cases, they do; in many cases, they don't. If they make the wrong decision, it affects the bottom line; it affects productivity, and it can affect the morale of a given department. The process of discharging the person is a long, drawn-out process; it is not employment-at-will in the sense that two days later you say you are going to fire them. There has to be a cause. There must be documentation and reasons for the discharge. It costs a company a lot more if they make a wrong decision.

HA: I know you are young, but you have seen a lot of things. I'm wondering, do you pull back when you know in your heart it will be a bad hire? Suppose a hiring manager has been looking for three months and is desperate, but you feel strongly that the candidate will not work out. What do you do?

ML: Well, I can only express my views, and certainly in my career, this has happened before. A quick example: I was interviewing for a senior marketing person who would report to the president of the organization. I felt the person had the skills, presented himself very well, but there was something missing. Upon checking references it was found that the person lied about his education, his degree. This was immediately brought to the president's attention, the person to whom he would report. It was my opinion that since this person did not tell the truth up front, I would not feel confident having this person handle the senior marketing position. The president did not care; he liked the candidate and wanted him. So against my advice, he hired the man. He was only with us a few months and left. Since I can only voice my opinion, in some situations, I ask for documentation, so if they turn against my opinion, and it comes back to bite them, there is a record that I gave my thoughts. It happens. No matter how great we think the candidate is, the candidate can go in and fall on his face during the interview with the hiring manager. It could be due to [a number of] reasons; it could be a bad day, or problems at home, or a motor vehicle accident before arriving that day. When one candidate interviewed with us, he was phenomenal. He went to the hiring manager and fell on his face. The hiring manager comes back and says he does not want this person. We say this person is great. We can only suggest; we are not the final decision. The hiring manager does not really like us, in recruiting, to tell them what to do 100 percent of the time. We can only give our views and opinions from what we evaluate at the interview.

HA: In interviewing candidates, do you find that different types of candidates fit into different types of positions?

ML: Yes, there are clearly some differences. Each profession has its own quirks. You will find, each kind of individual fits into a mold: Compassionate types are different from human resource types; engineering types are different from accounting types. If you recruit these people long enough, you will find each group has a little [idiosyncrasy] or a peculiarity about them. Many of your programmers' personalities are not like the accounting person, who is usually quite conservative. A sales person is an outgoing person and comes across that way. Each type of position creates its own set of requirements, and the individual personality comes with it.

HA: I know many people feel that the hire is complete when the person is brought on board. The fact of the matter is that if the person leaves three or five months later, just when they are hitting their stride, it can be very damaging to the organization in different ways. Could you elaborate on why retention is important, why excessive turnover is not good? What are some of your thoughts on retention and some of the best practices? Where does retention start, and how can you keep the best people in your organization?

ML: Retention begins on day one, the day the person actually comes in for the interview. If he or she gets through that process, the interview team and the hiring team complete the sale, the person buys into the sale and becomes an employee, and from that point forward it is retention. A definition of retention is how you treat the person the first day he or she is there, and how the person perceives what was discussed with him during the course of the interview, with the recruiting department or the hiring manager. If you are up front and honest, say what is actually there. If you sugar-coat it, you start off on the wrong foot. (e.g., I thought this was going to be here and now you tell me it is going to be this way. Your retention percentages go down and down.)

HA: In other words, what you say on the first day is the beginning of the person's impression of the organization. Was the equipment ready, the phone, desk, computer, or office/cubicle? In the first few weeks, the formative stages, people form very strong opinions of the organization.

ML: Yes, if things go wrong, it leaves a bad taste in one's mouth. If you have existing people around who may be negative, they could interact with a new employee. This could create negative feelings or apprehension in the new employee. If everything works out well in the first few months, it then becomes the responsibility of the person's supervisor or manager to start creating a positive environment. In this environment the new person feels wanted, is heard and is responded to. Whatever the needs he or she has that are legitimate and can be handled, should be appropriately given (e.g., a stronger light in the cubicle). If you meet the lesser requests of the new employee, it can help your retention in the long run. Showing an employee there is a career path available in the organization, showing that the company does listen, does respond, and has open channels of communication, is very important. You cannot base retention solely on monetary issues. There are many other issues: work life issues, commuting, time off, amenities that the company can provide (selling postage stamps in the cafeteria, laundry services). Companies furnish other amenities such as day care. I think you have to listen; each employee has a different urgency and a different desire. You cannot meet all of their requests by lumping them together. You can retain people by being a good listener, treat individuals as an individual, and listen to what is said and try to meet the general needs, if it is feasible and justifiable.

HA: What do you do when a highly prized employee resigns?

ML: As a supervisor, communicate with people on a consistent basis—how valuable they are to you, your team, your company, your department, and do it as often as possible, not on the day they leave. It means nothing to hear, "I really appreciate what you have been doing. I do not want you to leave; you're a valuable asset." That's the wrong time. If you had been listening prior to that, the employee would understand how valuable he is to the entire organization. Hopefully, he would want to stay or come to you if there was a problem when he was considering leaving. If there is open communication, hopefully, the employee will say, "I am having a problem that might cause me to leave." By hearing that, you, as supervisor, group leader, or manager can take steps to correct it.

HA: Would I be correct in making the following assumption? If an individual, of very high caliber, goes to his manager and says he is resigning, that manager probably did not do as good a job at managing that individual as he should have. There should have been some clue, in one way or another, that something was not right, or is that something that cannot be avoided and you are just caught off guard?

ML: Certainly you would say, as a good manager, one who has open communications and does have a feeling and understanding of each individual, would have some inkling of what is going on and some awareness of discord. But, in some situations there might be an introvert who doesn't talk or show his feelings, so the manager may not see it and doesn't come up with it. Part of being a good manager is the extra sensor that you have, that little voice that tells you something is not right with this employee, this individual is unhappy, and then approach the employee. It is not wrong for you as a manager to go to your employee and say

"Something is not right, what's wrong? Let's talk about it. Is there something we can do to correct it, or if it is strictly personal, I will stay out of the way, but if it has to do with work, let's talk and get it resolved."

HA: If you ask an employee why he is resigning and he tells you, "Well, I am getting $10,000 more in my next position," and if it is strictly a case of money, do you make a counteroffer?

ML: In my experience, counteroffers usually do not work over an extended period of time if the person's mind is set to leave. Their loyalty is out the door. Once they are upset, unless you can work out the issues, and make them understand their value, it is not going to change. You have to recognize, also, that turnover is good. Not [excessive] turnover, but you want some turnover in your company. It creates new ideas; it creates fresh thinking; it creates another way of looking at things, if something has been going on for an extended period of time. And sometimes it is good for the employee to move on, too. I don't think, that when I hire someone, I am hiring him or her through the retirement years. If I get a good three to five years out of someone I hire, I'm satisfied, and the manager should be satisfied, too. I don't think we hire people for retirement purposes, not in this year and age, we don't.

HA: Going to IBM when you are 22 and retiring when you are 52 is not the world we live in today.

ML: You will see that when you look at résumés. If you see someone at a job for five years, that is a long time. Most people stay a year or two years and then move on.

HA: So, you don't consider those people as job hoppers. You see them as managing their careers.

ML: Yes, if they are going from position "A" to position "B" to position "C" and it is a constant increase in responsibility and the learning of other skill sets along with what they pick up. If they are stagnant and just keep the same kind of job with lesser or the same responsibility, and don't pick up any additional knowledge, they are job-hopping. There are people out there that hop for the dollar, and no matter what you do, that's what they will do; nothing but the dollar will motivate these people. Unfortunately, they are out there.

HA: We have spoken about many things regarding planning, candidate generation, interviewing, and the kinds of people you hire. What about closing the deal? If there is someone the hiring manager really, really wants, what would you do to get this person on board? How do you help the hiring manager to say, "We did it! He signed the offer letter and he is coming on board"?

ML: Closing is important on both sides of the street, to the interviewer and the interviewee. Interviewing and finding a job is marketing. The applicants are selling themselves to you and you are selling your company to them. You sell the company. You tell him it is a good match; it is a good opportunity to take this position for his growth, for knowledge, for advancing his career. You sell the company on what it offers in the way of compensation, benefits, flexibility, lifestyle, and anything else that you think would be beneficial to entice the applicant to come in. On the other side, the applicant has to sell also. You ask for closure on both sides if you are extremely interested in the person.

HA: How important is speed for a company?

ML: In today's market speed is very important. If you get back to a candidate within 24 to 48 hours, he knows you are interested. If it lags on for a week, or ten days, or any period of time over 48 hours, you have a strong possibility, in today's climate, of losing that individual. I think it shows more aggressiveness on the part of the company if you do follow up within a 48-hour period. "We are interested, an offer is forthcoming, it will be there in a day or two, we are writing it to you, I hope you accept our offer, if you have any questions, get back to me." If you hold off and wait an extended period of time, the applicant will certainly be looking at other companies, and could get other offers presented to him. Delaying may make it appear that you are disorganized or you do not care. It is very important to get back to the candidate, if you are going to make an offer. I confer with my recruiters and once everyone agrees and the references are checked, this person is immediately called and he is given a verbal offer over the phone. If any negotiations are going to be done, it is going to be done before an offer is sent so we know when the offer goes out, the offer will be accepted.

HA: I am writing a chapter in my book called "Notes from the Underground." What are your thoughts, anything you ever wanted to say, whether it is regarding HR, employment relations, organizational development, behavior of people within an organization, senior management, leadership, or anything else? Now is the time to say what you wish.

ML: I think one thing I would like to elaborate on is interviewing. I made some notes to help me express myself. I think recruiting means to retain workers. But you have to retain workers from all generations. You have to keep up with the demand from each generation, and each generation has different requirements or different essentials they look for. For example, say you are talking to someone from the WWII generation. In that period of time, people were traditionalists. They are big on stability, big on security. If you go to the next generation, the Baby Boomers, they are a whole different type of person with some very different values. In my opinion, they are a generation that thrives on teamwork. Last, you have Generation X. They are a generation that says, "Show me the numbers." They need flexibility to work and to live. They do not want their jobs to be all encompassing. These are some of the things you must recognize in the people you are interviewing. If you understand each generation, not in 100 percent detail, but enough to know what they are looking for, how you communicate with each generation will help your recruiting.

B

Techniques for Staying Motivated During a Job Search

David H. Roper, author of Getting the Job You Want…Now! *and president of the Ascript Group (www.ascript.baweb.com) in Marblehead, Massachusetts, is a good friend, a superb résumé writer, and the best career counselor I have ever met. Upon visiting David's office, it is not possible to tell what colors the walls are because they are covered with hundreds of letters from people whose lives he turned around by rewriting their résumé, giving them advice, providing direction, and watching over them. His expertise, kindness, compassion, and ability to listen are legendary among his clients. If I were in trouble, David is the first person I would call. He wrote this chapter because, quite frankly, no one can do it as well.*

A job seeker is like a rock climber. Deep down, he competes with himself and confronts obstacle after obstacle along a route of great resistance. His success depends on his maintaining a delicate balance of focusing on the very step he is on, and constantly adhering to a master plan that he knows he must follow to reach the summit.

Bob Davis, a laid-off, high-tech channel marketing executive, was one job seeker who could identify with the rock climber. After several months of a steady slide from self-confidence before his layoff, to a deepening erosion of self-esteem because of his lack of progress, he knew his attitude and perspective *had* to change. Like the rock climber, he knew he must seek rewards in each small step that would move him along his path toward a job offer. So he made certain that each day had a quantifiable purpose, leading to his ultimate goal: a new job. Even the planning of the plan was a positive step toward his larger goal. Bob knew that the plan itself had to be realistically attainable, and the steps in the plan had to follow the path of least resistance. He forced himself to understand that attaining a job would come only after some struggling, disappointments, and rejection. He had to accept this as an inevitable part of the process, and only then could he go forward.

Understanding and Believing in the Odds

The job seeker, like the rock climber, first has to firmly believe in the feasibility of the plan. Otherwise he'll talk himself out of it. He won't endure. It is critical that he looks at relevant statistics and applies effort where the odds are best. For example, Bob learned that defining the target job and company, and proactively selling *to* it, gave him much better odds and a more viable plan than just waiting for available opportunities. He learned that advertised openings make up only about 10 percent of the hiring market, so if he were to exclusively concentrate on this method of job seeking, he would miss 90 percent of the market, the so-called "hidden market." Most employers plan to fill a position between 30 and 90 days *before* the actual position becomes available. So by targeting and selling to a job *ahead* of the actual opening, odds increase dramatically. Statistics show that the average job seeker over the age of 35 changes jobs every three years. This means that any single targeted position is likely to open up at least once every three years. So, if you target 100 companies, each with two positions you're seeking, you are looking at 200 qualified positions, or nearly six positions opening each month (200 divided by 36 months). Factor in a realistic 20 percent chance to win one of these openings *each month*, and the goals of your job search look much more attainable.

So how did Bob go about defining his target jobs and companies? First, he analyzed his skill sets and the markets they best fit, prioritizing the skills that he felt would give him the most leverage. He concentrated on his "hard" skills, those that meant immediate tangible value to a prospective employer. Bob defined some of his hard skills as sales forecasting via Excel, writing detailed marketing plans, and utilizing proven marketing channel contacts within his industry sector. Then he put himself in place of the reader of his résumé. He asked some key questions: How would I title myself? What am I, by title? What industry segment values me most? He knew he first needed to give himself a label. He had to define himself. Then he asked: If I were hiring someone for this title, knowing what I know about my field, what would be *my* true priorities and needs? What would *I* want to see? And what types of companies would I be in? Who would my reader be? What position level would feel the greatest need to see my résumé? He knew he didn't want to be a threat to the reader, so it had to be high enough above his level not to be intimidating, but low enough so he would be understood and valued. Then, via the Internet, he researched and defined the companies in his field that most closely resembled his profile. Voilà, his initial target marketing was in place.

Accumulating Rejection Is the Path to Success

The expert in all of us was once a beginner. And, unless we've been jobless on many occasions, we're beginners here, too. So we have to deal with failure as part of the process. Once we accept it, we're ready for it. We don't take it personally, but we accept it as part of the process. Ironically, in the job search, to fail often and quickly is the shortest path to winning. Since we've determined that the job search is a numbers game, we can safely say that by accumulating rejection, we'll get closer to acceptance.

If you're a job seeker, you can't let your emotions from past job experiences get in the way of the job search. It will hamper you and jeopardize your success. It is important to objectively analyze the culture of your past employer and your relationship with your former boss, so you can understand where you should and should not be with your future company and future boss. When you know what match to look for, you'll also know what is not acceptable. You'll then have fewer psychological setbacks when you do encounter rejection.

One of the techniques Bob Davis used to handle rejection was to hang a sign by his bathroom mirror which read "Babe Ruth struck out 1336 times in his career." He learned to make a game out of the process, reminding himself after a day of heavy rejection that he had, in fact, accomplished a lot. "I struck out 22 times today—used up 22 rejections in one day. "Terrific! I must be getting closer," he'd say. When times got particularly tough, he hung up his accomplishments list next to the Babe Ruth sign. It was his list of accomplishments he was proud of—what he'd achieved in the face of adversity. It served as a reminder of times when he could have given up, but didn't.

True, rejection during a job search is no fun, and the ramifications of not getting a job are potentially disastrous. It can be helpful for job seekers to find support in others in similar situations, to help them through seemingly endless rejection. Beyond the practical wisdom gained from others' job search experiences, it helps to know there are people just like you who are having the same problems. These days, we're seeing increasing numbers of non-profits such as churches, colleges, and community counseling centers rallying to serve as catalysts and facilitators for job-seeker groups. Being in a group gives the job searcher somewhere to go, something to look forward to. It keeps morale up.

So how do we know when and if the job search will end? We don't know when. But neither does the rock climber, though he can see the summit, just as we can picture the job we deserve. We know that by setting short-term, attainable goals, and by working the best odds, we are constantly taking little steps that are goal-oriented, steps that are accomplishments in themselves.

Understanding the Value of a Hectic Schedule

Bob set up and strictly adhered to a daily job search schedule. He needed to fulfill the daily goals he had set in order not to fail. On days when the going got tough, he sometimes reviewed the big picture, the statistics, the master plan. He sometimes went back to the Babe Ruth sign, and to the accomplishments list. As a way to force himself to be objective and to make certain his goal was realistic, he'd sometimes ask himself "If I were hiring me, would I?" He made certain that his daily schedule was properly designed to be both efficient and to maintain motivation throughout the day. He planned the best times for exercise and relaxation (usually after two hours of heavy cold calling, when a reward was needed). He planned the best hours for research, letter writing, creative strategizing, networking, etc. He gave the schedule balance, variety, and structure, which could carry him from one step to the next without jeopardizing his motivation. In short, he made his schedule demanding, like a good, well-balanced job. In fact, at times Bob's schedule worked so well at productively filling his time that he became anxious that there wasn't enough time in the day to meet his goals. Terrific! Slightly overworked people work slightly better.

When we have schedules, we are more structured. When we are more structured, we become more productive. When we are productive, we stay motivated. Time goes faster. More leads generate more leads, more contacts generate more contacts, more ideas generate more letters, more research generates more knowledge, and knowledge generates value. Value, ultimately, generates jobs.

Keeping Your Self-Esteem Highly Esteemed

In the face of rejection, we need to hold together our self-esteem. This means being creative about magnifying our strengths and our value, even in our everyday environment. Like spotlessly shining the car inside and out. Or perfecting a craft or hobby to the point of recognized excellence. Or feeling pride for repairing the dishwasher. Or dressing well, even if we're just going to the library to do some research. By looking as though we feel good about ourselves, we'll increase our odds that others will see more value in us as well. If we compete with ourselves to look better, act better, work harder, and think smarter, we will emerge victorious. In the final analysis, it is our choice.

Put yourself, as Bob Davis did, up there with the rock climber, with only two ways to go. Up there on that wall of rock where you can't look back and every little move you make can be its own small success. Put yourself where every new step can be an opportunity to excel, one that will move you slowly, but inevitably, toward the summit.

Index

INTERNATIONAL CONTACT INFORMATION

AUSTRALIA
McGraw-Hill Book Company Australia Pty. Ltd.
TEL +61-2-9417-9899
FAX +61-2-9417-5687
http://www.mcgraw-hill.com.au
books-it_sydney@mcgraw-hill.com

CANADA
McGraw-Hill Ryerson Ltd.
TEL +905-430-5000
FAX +905-430-5020
http://www.mcgrawhill.ca

GREECE, MIDDLE EAST,
NORTHERN AFRICA
McGraw-Hill Hellas
TEL +30-1-656-0990-3-4
FAX +30-1-654-5525

MEXICO (Also serving Latin America)
McGraw-Hill Interamericana Editores S.A. de C.V.
TEL +525-117-1583
FAX +525-117-1589
http://www.mcgraw-hill.com.mx
fernando_castellanos@mcgraw-hill.com

SINGAPORE (Serving Asia)
McGraw-Hill Book Company
TEL +65-863-1580
FAX +65-862-3354
http://www.mcgraw-hill.com.sg
mghasia@mcgraw-hill.com

SOUTH AFRICA
McGraw-Hill South Africa
TEL +27-11-622-7512
FAX +27-11-622-9045
robyn_swanepoel@mcgraw-hill.com

UNITED KINGDOM & EUROPE
(Excluding Southern Europe)
McGraw-Hill Publishing Company
TEL +44-1-628-502500
FAX +44-1-628-770224
http://www.mcgraw-hill.co.uk
computing_neurope@mcgraw-hill.com

ALL OTHER INQUIRIES Contact:
Osborne/McGraw-Hill
TEL +1-510-549-6600
FAX +1-510-883-7600
http://www.osborne.com
omg_international@mcgraw-hill.com